*Seek success
and
laugh
through the whole adventure!*

Setting the vision and drawing your blueprint

Understanding value and marketing your practice

Creating a wonderful environment

Customizing systems to function effectively

Ensuring your practice is strong

Securing your financial health

Satisfying your personal and professional needs

What Others Are Saying....

I inspire people to chase after their dreams and live a life uncommon, and now I have an excellent resource to help them make it happen. Dr. Linda Hancock's new book, ***Open for Business Success***, serves as a guide for anyone who finally wants to make their dream a reality.
- Kelly Croy
Inspirational Speaker, Author & Performance Artist
www.KellyCroy.com

Linda is a first-rate person, a first-rate psychologist, and a first-rate business-woman. But her brightest-shining trait is her benevolence in generously sharing each of these with people fortunate enough to cross paths with her. As I have begun establishing my own private practice, Linda has been a priceless Godsend, offering me encouragement, inspiration, and handfuls of those little rib-jabbing ideas that can really get things going in building your private practice.
• Greg Godard, M.C., R. Psych.

I have been doing Linda's Income Tax and government remittances for the past several years and am always impressed by her savvy business practices. She deals with everything from the tiny administrative details to large marketing campaigns with efficiency and ease. And through it all, she always knows her exact financial situation. This business woman knows what it takes to operate a profitable business!
• Lola Herter
Lo Tax Accounting and Tax, Medicine Hat, AB

Linda has taken a business which would normally be housed in one building to a worldwide audience through social media. She has learned how to apply Internet marketing concepts to build websites, publish articles and network with individuals. This not only has helped her to expand her speaking and writing activities but also attracts new clients for her private practice on a regular basis.

    • Tom Antion
    http://www.GreatInternetMarketingTraining.com

Linda has an excellent way of networking with others and using resources in the community. She makes a point of meeting professionals and learning about what services they offer. She is also willing to share her expertise with others and the result is that everyone benefits!

    • Marie Ziegler
    Insolvency Administrator

Dr. Linda is full of life and passionate about helping others. Her books, presentations and interviews are filled with wisdom, humour and easy-to-understand strategies for both personal and business growth.

    • Wayne Kelly
    "The Radio Guy"
    www.onairpublicity.com

For the last few years I have watched Dr. Linda build her private practice into a strong business. She has always been diligent about researching options and has not been afraid to try out new ideas. As a dentist and a businessman I have learned that it is important to balance good customer service with healthy self-care. She also not only understands this but demonstrates it in her own life.

    • Brad C. Lien DDS

For five years Linda has written a newspaper column entitled "All Psyched Up" which is published on a weekly basis. As her editor I am pleased to state that she offers practical and sound advice for the readers. With Linda's advice people will have the tools for success in their personal and professional lives.

    • Chris Brown
    Associate Editor Medicine Hat News

There are so many things that you need to learn to build a successful business. I have known Linda for over twenty years, and have watched her learn, grow, and explore. Her perspective is unique, and her approach is challenging. Linda has a radical view of how to combine your personal and business life and be successful at both. Her many years of life experience come into focus in this exciting new book.

• Gordon Ashdown, Founder and Owner of
Can-West Wholesale Esthetics Supplies
http://www.canwestesthetics.com

I had the privilege of working closely with Dr. Linda Hancock on the Board of Directors of the Cypress Club in 2004-2006 while I was President of the Club. This organization had been established in 1903 by area business professionals, bankers, political leaders and ranchers. Dr. Hancock worked diligently to develop a concise Business Plan for the Club establishing a clear direction for the board to follow in building on the success of this historical institution. Through her professional knowledge and abilities combined with her vision and passion, the Cypress Club is in a strong position today to continue on in its legacy in the Medicine Hat business area.

• Mark Dumanowski, B.Comm., CIM, F.C.S.I.
Vice-President & Investment Advisor
Portfolio Manager
CIBC Wood Gundy - Medicine Hat, AB.
(Past President of the Cypress Club, 2004-2006)

As the 2009 Small Business of the Year (Medicine Hat & District Chamber of Commerce) I take great pride in my business operations. Creating a support system that I can trust was key to my business development, and surrounding myself with respected individuals like Dr. Linda was priority number one. I have faith in Dr. Linda's business acumen, and her lessons and insight are suitable for both business and personal success! Her knowledge and passion are pure magic to me!

• Trevor Moore, Professional Magician
The Magic & Comedy of Trevor Moore
www.magicoftrevormoore.com

Also by Dr. Hancock:

Life is an Adventure
…every step of the way!

Loving Your Life
Learning from the Past, Living in the Present and
Looking Forward to the Future

Workplace Bullying
Workplace Bettering

Divorce:
Decision-Making with Dignity

All Psyched Up

For more information view Dr. Hancock's websites:

www.lindahancock.com

Open for Business Success

A professional approach
for building your practice

Open for Business Success

A professional approach
for building your practice

DR. LINDA HANCOCK

Order this book online at www.trafford.com
or email orders@trafford.com

Most Trafford titles are also available at major online book retailers.

Printed in the United States of America.

ISBN: 978-1-4269-5086-5 (sc)
ISBN: 978-1-4269-5087-2 (hc)
ISBN: 978-1-4269-5088-9 (e)

Library of Congress Control Number: 2010918400

Trafford rev. 12/29/2010

 www.trafford.com

North America & international
toll-free: 1 888 232 4444 (USA & Canada)
phone: 250 383 6864 ♦ fax: 812 355 4082

This Book is Dedicated to....

Those who have helped me to learn about myself, business and the world

and

Those who state that they are thirsty to learn from me.

Foreword

I first met Dr. Linda Hancock about eight or nine years ago when she was a participant in the workshop I was presenting. Little did I know at the time that I was contributing several hours of training to a woman who probably has the highest number of years of education of anyone I have ever met. (She attended university classes alone over a period of twenty-two years!)

Linda asked me to lunch because she was interested in continuing her life-long learning and enhancing her career by becoming a Registered Psychologist. Years previous to this, one of my mentors – a strong and astute woman, not unlike Linda – said to me that if someone wants something and asks you to lunch to discuss it, they should pay. Following this advice, when the bill arrived, I therefore passed it over to Linda. She has never let me forget this!

Since we met I have watched Linda complete two degrees (after her initial two degrees), finish her licensing requirements to become a Registered Psychologist and start a private practice that has grown to one of the most successful in our region. I have also watched with interest as she expanded her practice into areas that psychologists rarely consider in their work.

Today, Linda is a successful psychologist, speaker and business woman. This is a statement that might seem simple and obvious but bears repeating. Linda is both successful psychologist AND a successful business woman. I believe that many of us do well in one or the other but not in both. Because I am viewed in a similar manner I am often asked by others to help them develop their business practices. I conclude every consultation with the words, "Now, if you want to see an example of a successful psychologist, go and book time with Linda and find out how she does what she does."

What you have in your hands is a book that may seem to be deceptively like common sense. If it was merely common sense, however, you wouldn't need to have the book in your hands! Don't let the practical nature of the book fool you. The advice is sound and contains both knowledge and strategies that will help you to build a strong and successful business for yourself – without having to learn the hard way!

Follow the advice between these covers. It is the next best thing to having Linda coach you. And when you are done reading (and re-reading) this book, "Go and schedule time with Linda to further find out how she does what she does."

Paul Jerry, M.A., R. Psych., Ph.D.
Associate Professor, Applied Psychology
Athabasca University
Psychologist in Independent Practice

Table of Contents

Chapter Three
CREATING A WONDERFUL ENVIRONMENT   69

Chapter Four
CUSTOMIZING SYSTEMS TO FUNCTION
EFFECTIVELY   97

Chapter Seven
SATISFYING YOUR PERSONAL AND PROFESSIONAL

Introduction

Starting or developing a private practice for solo professionals

Frequently individuals study in their field for many years with a plan of starting a private practice in order to use those knowledge and skills. There are many things, however, about business that are never taught to these professionals to prepare them and despite their passion for a new venture, problems can arise in several areas.

My plan for SUCCESS encompasses seven specific areas of business that each need to be considered and implemented in order to do well. Whether you are an individual who is starting a business for the very first time or someone who has been practicing for many years, the principles in this book will help you to think about how you can do things in a manner that is faster, easier and more beneficial for you and your client.

Setting the vision and drawing your blueprint for the business will greatly help you to clearly identify exactly what type(s) of services you will offer and how they will be provided. This includes describing your "ideal" client, deciding the scope of your practice and setting financial goals.

You will need to consider practical issues such as the location where you will practice and the hours your office will be open. I don't think anyone would consider building a house without having a detailed blueprint. Your business blueprint involves planning for a business that will facilitate building a practice that you and your clients will love for many years to come.

Understanding value and marketing your practice. As a solo professional you are an entrepreneur who is totally responsible for the entire business. In order to develop an effective marking plan you will need to identify what makes your services unique and how you can add value for the client. Studying the competition will help you to know what is offered in your area and allow you to consider the need for your specific services. You may wish to consider collaborating with other professionals in order to share expenses or meet market needs. It is important to have referral sources which can be developed through offline techniques such as advertising including creation of brochures and business cards. You may also develop contacts through community service such as speaking for groups teaching a college course or writing a newspaper column. On-line marketing might be done in the form of offering teleseminars, providing Internet consulting services or writing for article directories. ·

Creating a wonderful environment. If you will be at the office for most of your waking hours, it is important that you are comfortable and happy with your surroundings. You and your clients will benefit if the location and parking or transit options are convenient. Handicapped access and bathroom facilities are important considerations as are arrangements for evening hour appointments. Decorate your office as a reflection of your personality. Choosing colours and furniture that are suitable to your taste and the type of client you will serve will be appreciated by all. You do not need to follow the example of all the other professionals but can make the environment unique. Creating a healthy environment also includes ensuring that any staff you have are friendly and efficient. First impressions start with the first voice that the client hears. ·

Customizing systems to function effectively. You will need to have a plan for how filing and bookkeeping practices will be operationalized. Choosing computer software and ensuring that staff knows how to use it properly will save many hours at year end. You will need to develop processes for taking new referrals, negotiating contracts and communicating with clients, staff and others. Systems involve having an effective plan for doing things which can be easily repeated over and over again with good results.

Ensuring your practice is strong means that you will need to work with confidence in your area of competency and in collaboration with your professional association. In order to obtain and maintain a license to operate your practice you must be knowledgeable and able to fulfill the Standards of Practice for your regulatory body. Understanding how to provide ethical, confidential service and resolve formal complaints will not only save you time, stress and money but also protect your reputation. Professional Development opportunities and renewal of certifications will enhance your skills and knowledge which, in turn, add value for the client.

Securing your financial health. One of the most important things you will do to ensure success is prepare a Business Plan. This will provide you with clarity and a blueprint for your practice. Banking services and credit can be adjusted each year according to the financial statements that are prepared by your accountant. It is important that your receipts are greater than your expenditures so you can enjoy growth and experience financial health. One of the problems that can greatly harm businesses is when accounts receivables are not collected in a timely fashion You are responsible for the financial well-being of your business and you may therefore need to take a very small salary for the first few months of operation and then increase it as your profit grows. You may also benefit from hiring staff on a part-time or contract basis or do without any staff until the business is established.

Satisfying your personal and professional needs. Because you are the solo professional you only have income if and when you are working. You therefore need to ensure that you are rested and healthy. Support from other professionals will help you to learn how to deal with stressful situations and discuss options to deal with problems. It is important that you feel optimistic about your new venture. Enjoying your work will encourage you to be at the office so you need to ensure that what you do feeds your soul. Ensuring that you have a work and personal balance will also help you to maintain good perspective. Many professionals add a couple of days of touring to professional development opportunities so that they can build their skills and contacts, obtain a tax deduction and also take a break in an interesting environment

Using this SUCCESS theory will help you to plan and assess your private practice and then make the adjustments you need in order to ensure that you, your staff and your clients are all having their needs met in a healthy manner.

Remember, this is YOUR business. You have the option to be creative!

Chapter One

SETTING THE VISION AND DRAWING YOUR BLUEPRINT

Why private practice?

Sometimes it is difficult to decide whether to work for an employer or to start your own private practice. There are advantages and disadvantages for each of these choices. Your decision will likely be made based on your personality, goals and the opportunities that are available.

For many years, I worked for the government. In 2006 I hired a Business Manager to help me decide whether I should stay in that employment or expand my part-time private practice into a full-time endeavor. There were many things to consider before making any changes as the government job offered set hours, guaranteed income with regular raises in pay, ongoing professional development and specific benefits including a pension plan as well as a benefit plan to cover illness, health and dental costs.

I had been raised in a home where having security was valued. Everyone talked about and looked forward to the retirements they had planned and invested in throughout their careers. There was a general consensus that a government pension plan was the best you could get. And although most of my family members lived to healthy old ages, there was a good feeling in knowing that I had casual illness coverage as well as a short and long-term disability plans.

I really didn't want to give up the pension plan and benefits but, at the same time, thought that I could likely match or better my income if I was in business for myself and I really wanted the opportunity to create a business that would reflect my values and dreams.

The newly-hired Business Manager asked me to ask for a copy of my pension plan portfolio and speak with the company representative about my options.

I requested statements that would outline the pension income I could receive by retiring at ages 55, 60 and 65 years and was shocked to learn that despite my years of service and the regular contributions that I had made, my retirement income was what I will term "pitiful" even if I worked until I was 65 years of age!

I took out a calculator and started to work the numbers.

The hourly fee that I could charge in private practice was almost triple my hourly rate of pay in the government job. If I paid myself a salary and reserved about seventeen percent of gross income for coverage of my government employee remittances, I would still have plenty of money to purchase health and dental coverage and also make investments which would be available to fund my retirement years.

I knew that there would be risks in setting out on my own. If I was ill enough to be away from the office there wouldn't be any income. I would need to pay for my own professional development opportunities and, at the same time, would lose income while I was away in order to attend them. As well, I knew that I would not have the "protection" that comes with having a supervisor and other people with whom I could consult about difficult cases. Instead of having an office and equipment provided for me, I would have to pay all the costs for rent, utilities, advertising, and the numerous other expenses that are associated with running a private practice.

At the same time, I wanted the freedom that comes with operating a business and being my own boss.

One of the things that helped me make my decision was to list all the concerns that I had on paper and then gather information about how I might deal with each of them in a private practice setting. The research involved talking with other professionals who were already in private practice, reading articles about specific options, consulting with companies that offered benefit plans and considering investment opportunities that could replace my pension plan.

It only took a couple of months for me to realize that I could let go of the security that I thought I had in my job in order to set up and develop my business. After serious consideration, I decided to leave the government job with all of its guarantees and "perks". I haven't looked back since.

Oh, there have been times when I have had to give myself a "pep talk" for spending too much or not seeing as many clients as I needed to in order to reach my goals but, the rewards have far exceeded the fears that I once felt.

Making a decision to go into a private practice can be a difficult one, especially if you are worried about giving up your benefits or about not having a regular guaranteed income. Your personality style and your situation in life are factors that will affect your decision-making and ultimately guide you in this area.

What are the things that concern you about operating a private practice? Do you think you could handle the pressure of being your own boss and taking responsibility for the business and your own future?

Ensure that you have enough information to allay your concerns before you begin and then you probably will not be facing days that could be filled with regret.

Consider the things that you will gain by having your own business. Are the advantages greater than the demands? Will they outweigh the list of things that you might have to give up in your present situation?

You see, building a business takes work and, if you are going to invest time and energy into it, you need to make sure that you know why you are doing it. The "why" is what keeps you going – even in the difficult times! Know your "why" and be able to state it clearly to yourself and others. Then you will be able to move forward with confidence.

What is your vision?

Many websites including *Industry Canada* describe vision as "what a company wants to be. It focuses on tomorrow; it is inspirational; it provides clear decision-making criteria; and it is timeless".

In order to start or develop your business, you need to have a very clear picture of what you want your practice to look like in the future and have a blueprint prepared which will guide you as you build it. But that blueprint is really the expansion of a philosophy or purpose that you should be able to state in a few well-chosen words. The vision is not for the public but for you and your staff to use as a focus.

Some businesses and organizations prepare a mission statement which describes how the company is at the time of writing. Mission statements usually identify the clients, processes and level of performance - things which have been accomplished already. New businesses do not have this, and therefore need to start with preparing a vision for the future.

Whether you are starting a new business or working at improving an established one, the first thing you should do is make sure that the company vision accurately describes your hopes and plans for the future.

When I was in graduate school we were asked by a professor to write a personal philosophy of life. It took a great deal of thought and editing in order to create exactly what I wanted in one short sentence. When I was finished, however, I knew very clearly that this philosophy would be one which I would use not only for my business but also for my entire life. It reads "To live and learn and love in a manner that will lead to personal growth and enhance the lives of others".

When I opened my part-time practice, I decided to add a statement to the Philosophy which would make the task even clearer. It read "My goal is to encourage individuals, groups, organizations and communities to reach their potential".

You see, if you don't know your values and heart's desires, it is hard to develop a business or build a life that will accomplish them.

Whatever statement you create must reflect your values and dreams - for as the solo professional YOU ARE THE BUSINESS. Make sure that each word in your statement is carefully chosen and has meaning.

You will be printing these statements on your brochures and marketing materials and quoting them with pride whenever someone asks you about your business. Think about how you will gain confidence and respect from others for knowing where you are headed and being able to verbalize it!

A vision statement is very important because it not only names your destination but also serves as a reminder that you are on the right path in order to reach it!

Drawing your blueprint

Imagine what would happen if you decided to build a house without a blueprint? The hired contractor wouldn't know what to do. You would not be able to order the necessary materials because you wouldn't know what you needed or how much. You wouldn't even know where to start on the project.

Often clients tell me that they would like to travel, study or complete a project. When I ask them about how and when they will do this, they reply "I don't know." Apathy and lack of planning usually result in lack of accomplishment.

The same thing occurs for those who are starting or developing a business. If you don't have a blueprint, you won't know where to start let alone be able to build a strong practice.

I strongly believe that more time and effort needs to be invested into planning the work than in actually doing the work and agree with the many successful people who state "You need to work harder ON the business than IN the business".

One of the things that I learned to do several years ago was to write a Business Plan. The Internet offers a great deal of information to help you create one as well as different templates which can be completed in manageable sections. You will be challenged to think about the market, your competition, marketing strategies and the unique ways that you can serve your clientèle. Actually the key to success in writing the Business Plan is the fact that it makes you THINK about what you want to do and how you will do it.

Business Plans also force you to develop financial awareness.

You will be required to list all of the expenses which you will incur during the year and then calculate how much income will be needed to pay all of them. Owning a business means that you are responsible for paying your bills and earning an appropriate living so don't forget to add in the amount that you want to personally take out of the business for yourself.

If you want to build a strong and successful business, you need to make a number of decisions that have a financial component. Where will you house your business? Who will you serve? How often will you do that? How will you attract clients? What will you charge? What are the risks?

Once you can clearly state exactly how you want the business to function you will be able to lay out a list of tasks to accomplish in each category of the Business Plan. One task, under Marketing, for example, might be to have an advertisement in the telephone book. This task can be broken down further into smaller pieces. Who will research the costs, write the ad and decide where and how it will be published? How will this be paid – monthly, quarterly or yearly?

Just because you are a solo professional, doesn't mean that you need or should do everything. You might seek help for some of the tasks through a contract worker, virtual assistant or by asking for the support of a good friend. Usually it is worthwhile to pay a few dollars to someone who is an expert in a specific area rather than struggle or risk doing an unprofessional job. For example, hiring copywriters to prepare marketing materials will likely increase your profit as they know how to word things to attract clients. While they are working on this project, you can be seeing more clients and it won't take very long until you have earned enough to pay for their services!

When you know who will be doing a task, when it will be done and how it will be paid for, you are living in a proactive rather than reactive manner. This not only feels good, but also helps you to accomplish things in a more timely fashion.

Developing your business plan needs to also consider your personal needs. As a solo professional, your business depends on your own heath. You are the employer and the employee so you need to make sure that you have incorporated self-care practices into your plan.

For example, I know that massages are good for my health and therefore make sure that they are scheduled for twice a month at least three months in advance so I never have to worry about calling in and being told that my massage therapist is too booked to see me! I also have all the appointments entered into my business calendar as they are booked so I never have to cancel because of a client appointment or meeting.

Developing a blueprint for your business requires a great deal of thought and work but offers huge rewards as it takes most of the stress out of your day!

I recommend that before you ever open the door to your business, you work ON your business by laying out a clear and detailed plan for at least a year in advance. That will help to ensure that working IN your business is a pleasant adventure with few unwanted surprises.

(And, of course, each year will be easier as you will have accurate financial records and valuable experience which you can use to develop the next year's Business Plan).

What's in a name?

One of the most important things that each of us has is our name. Frequently, I ask groups of people to tell the 'story' of how they were given their first, middle and surnames and the feelings that they have about the naming process and the name itself.

Deciding on a name for your business is also very important and there are a number of things to consider before you settle on one. Some of these include:

1. **The type of business that you have established -** If you incorporate or register a limited company, you may wish to indicate that in the name of the business. For example, my business is *Dr. Linda Hancock Inc.*

2. **Whether you want your own name included in the business name** - Some professionals use their full name in the title or use initials and their surname. *Paul Jerry Consulting* or *P.A. Jerry Consulting* are examples.

3. **If you want to expand your business in the future you might want to choose a name that will allow for this.** I have set up a speaking and product business named *Hancock and Associates* which leaves room for other people without naming them.

4. **When you want to name the business after a city or region** - *Medicine Hat Dental Clinic* allows the client to know where the practice is located.

5. **Perhaps you would like to include a symbolic word or descriptive term** - For example, *Phoenix Safe House* was created by individuals who wanted to offer encouragement to abuse victims as the Phoenix is a bird that, according to legend, rises from the ashes.

6. **Allow for the possibility that you might sell or leave the business to someone else.** You might want to name your business with a generic term that can be used by anyone who takes over in the future. *Family Psychological Services*, for example, is a name that could be used even if you are no longer with the business.

The name that you have for your business offers the client a first impression of you. It therefore should be easy to remember, easy to spell, offer meaning and be one that you will display with pride on your office door, business card and letterhead.

The relationship that you and your client begin together usually starts with them knowing your name and the name you have given your business. It is therefore important that you use the same thought and care that you did when naming your children

What is competency?

Professional organizations are usually concerned that their members have ongoing competency in their chosen are of work. This means that they have the knowledge, skills and abilities to do what they say they will do with expertise and confidence. Private practitioners therefore need to create a professional development plan that will allow them to continually learn and grow.

Competency is usually established and verified by the regulatory body before a professional is licensed to open private practice but it is the professional's responsibility to ensure that competency is maintained by developing a learning plan each year.

There are five things that need to be considered regarding competency when you are preparing your plan:

1. **Identify areas to adopt, improve, or enhance** - First of all, decide the areas in which you would like to be classed as competent. There might be a different area of practice that you wish to adopt or a new service that you would like to add to your list of client services. Perhaps there are specific techniques or even technologies that you think would improve your practice if you could gain competency with them. You might wish to research new theories or methods. Maybe you think that your professionalism would be enhanced by learning about a new business model or by creating products to assist your clientele.

2. **Consider the ways that you might learn about the specific area you have chosen** - Is there a course or workshop in which you could learn about this? Would a convention of your professional organization offer opportunities for you to gain the information you are seeking? Maybe you could talk with others in your field and ask for suggestions about how to pursue your goals for professional development. The Internet is a good place to learn about opportunities where you can network, research and study or it might even offer you the specific information you are seeking about your topic.

3. **Arrange internships, practicums or supervised practice** - Many times expertise is best developed through observation and hands-on experience. I know a psychologist who worked in a law office for a whole year in order to learn about separation and divorce and to prepare himself in order to be recognized as an Expert Witness in the Justice system. Watching an expert work and then having that expert watch you duplicate the procedure is a wonderful way to not only gain knowledge but also develop or improve your own skill level.

4. **Prepare a written learning plan** - When you put your professional development plan in writing there is a much higher possibility that you will complete all of your learning goals as this will help to keep you accountable. Be very clear in defining your desired outcomes

and expected completion dates. File your learning plans in a binder so that they are easy to access at any time and review at year end.

5. **Begin** - Nothing happens until there is action. Even a small step forward will put your closer to achieving your goals.

6. **Schedule a regular evaluation** - It is important that you review your learning plan several times throughout the year. Make adjustments when necessary and remember to celebrate your accomplishments.

Competency is not only a professional requirement for your practice license but also a way to boost your self-esteem. When you are learning and growing, you feel better about yourself and the services that you have to offer your clients.

A learning plan also keeps you out of trouble.

Imagine being scheduled for brain surgery and then finding out that the doctor is a gynecologist? I'm sure you wouldn't want to enter the operating room, would you? It's the same with your clients. They want to enter your office knowing that you are able to help them with the problems that they have. That means that you should have the appropriate knowledge, skills and abilities in that specific problem area. If you don't, you face the risk of harming your client and having a formal complaint lodged against you.

Before you open the door, make sure that your competency and the client's needs are a good match. When you do this, you will find that both you and the client will do well.

Who is your client?

When you are starting or developing your business, it is important that you are able to identify those who would be your ideal clients. Write out a profile of the client needs you can competently address and then you will be clear about how to market and screen referrals appropriately.

It is not ethical or practical to try to serve everyone in a society and you therefore not only need to identify who your client will be but also who you will not serve.

Clients need to know that you have credentials as well as the ability to help them with their problem. Do not allow them to talk you into seeing them if you feel that you are not the right match no matter how convincing or desperate they seem to be.

Assess your areas of competency. What skills, abilities and supervision have you acquired that allow you to claim expertise and confidence in a specific area of practice? Your education should prepare you through in-depth study and your internship or practicum should provide you with working experience in that area.

There are several things that you need to consider when identifying the ideal client for your area of competency:

1. **Age** - Do you want your business to serve children, adolescents, adults or seniors? Do you have the training to work with that age group?

2. **Gender** - Are your services going to be best suited for males or females?

3. **Units** - Will you be working with individuals, families, groups, organizations or communities?

4. **Ability to pay** – Who has coverage or can afford your fees?

5. **Scope of practice** - Is there a particular niche that you will be serving?

6. **Exclusion**s - Who or what types of problems will you not serve? Do you know why you have come to this conclusion?

Once you have identified who your ideal clients are, you will be able to create a suitable environment in which to serve and a marketing plan to attract them. For example, my office is best suited for adults and my marketing plan is designed primarily to target clients from self or company and insurance referrals. In contrast, a therapist who works with children would likely establish a completely different type of office setting and would then develop marketing suitable for parents or organizations who deal with the children.

When you start a new business and are depending on the income to pay your bills, it is tempting to accept every referral you receive. This is not practical or ethical and, in fact, can harm your business. On the other hand, when you only accept referrals for those who fit into your ideal client profile, their needs will be met, you will both experience a degree of satisfaction and your reputation as a competent professional will be guaranteed.

Dr. Linda Hancock

Where will you locate?

Real estate agents claim that the most important thing to consider when setting up your residence or business is "location, location, location". Before you actually select the address where you will work, you will need to consider several things.

Country - We live in a world that seems to be shrinking due to modern transportation and technological advances. You may decide to start your business in a country other than the one where you are now living or provide services to clients in other countries through the Internet.

Even though this is possible and may seem rather simple to do, take time to ensure that you meet all appropriate work visa and licensing requirements for the countries where you will provide services. You may need to hire a lawyer to help you prepare the appropriate documentation. Make sure you have an estimate of the costs before you begin so that you don't end up with debts and regret.

You will also need to consider the difficulties that might occur if the new culture and economy are not be as receptive as your own country to the services you have to offer.

Remember also that moving from your professional and personal supports may be difficult, especially if you do not have someone to help you through the stress that can be associated with starting a new business.

Region - You will need to research the requirements for practicing in the area that you are considering. There may be governmental or professional expectations to fulfill before you can work in the new region. It is likely wise NOT to lease, rent or buy any property until you meet the requirements and have all the appropriate documentation to operate your business in your possession.

Community - Each community has its own combination of economic, ethnic and cultural influences. Consider the attitudes that the residents of the community may hold towards your profession. Some cultures, for example, are not open to dealing with professionals and instead meet their needs through consultation with friends or family.

What competition would you encounter in the community where you are hoping to practice? Are there other agencies or professionals with whom you can partner? Are you comfortable enough and feel that this will be a safe and welcoming place to begin your practice? You will need to be contented from both business and personal perspectives so take time to do enough research to determine that all your needs will be met after you have moved into the community but before you begin acting on your plan.

Building – Your office must be convenient for both you and your clients. There are several different options to consider before establishing your business location.

If you have never secured an office before, especially if you are planning to buy one, it is wise to take someone who is familiar with construction and business with you for viewings. That person will be objective and may save you from a lot of grief by pointing out structural problems with the building or other factors that might interfere with your business goals. You will be thankful, for example, if you friend notices and warns you about nearby railway tracks - especially if you are hoping for a peaceful spa-like setting!

Ensure that there is transit nearby as well as suitable parking for you and your clients. Consider special needs such as wheelchair accessibility and bathroom convenience.

And remember, if any renovations are needed, that they seldom are completed in the timeframe quoted by contractors. As a result, you may not be able to open the business on the date you planned and this will result in lost income. One of my friends was to open her dental therapy office in November but the site was not ready for clients until the following spring! She paid a significant price both financially and emotionally.

Other things to consider regarding your office space include the costs for utilities, taxes and ongoing repairs. Ensure that you are diligent in your research efforts so that you are not surprised by any unexpected costs.

Ask for a written contract and read it carefully before you move anything into the office or advertise your location.

Perhaps another professional will rent some space in their office to you. You may even be able to pay a little extra for the use of their office equipment and receptionist services.

On the other hand, you might be able to rent or purchase a facility and then sub-let your space to other business professionals. For four years, for example I arranged my hours so that I could rent my office for a few hours each week to another psychologist. We shared the monthly expenses equally even though he wanted the space for less than half of the month. This cut down on my costs but also allowed me to enjoy the benefits of having a permanent office setting.

I was also able to negotiate a reduced office rent by agreeing to sign a three-year lease and do some painting in the office.

There is great freedom in knowing that I am able to cover the entire office costs each month with the income generated in only a half day of seeing clients. You see, the last thing you want is to have so many expenses that you are pressured to take on more work than you can handle or have to give up income that would otherwise be yours to enjoy.

Choosing a location for your business can be an adventure that leads to either bad flashbacks or pleasant memories. Make sure you take your time and consider the strengths and weaknesses of each option that is available to you. It is better to slow down and use caution than to live with regrets.

What tone are you setting?

There are many definitions for the word "tone" but, when describing a business it refers to the general atmosphere of a place or situation and the effect that it has on people. Your goal should be to provide an environment that is comfortable and attractive for you and your clients.

Let's just use the five senses to describe how good tone can be found in an environment:

SIGHT - Even before clients arrive at your doorstep they have started to form an opinion.

The neighbourhood where you are located, the condition of the outside of the building and even the other people who are standing in the area impact the impression that they will have of you and your business.

Consider how you would feel if you went to see a professional and had to walk past piles of garbage that were stacked by the door. Now imagine the difference if you were walking along a walkway bordered by flowers and trimmed shrubs?

The cleanliness of your office, colours of walls and furniture as well as the paperwork that you give to the client all help to set the tone for your office.

Oh, and don't forget that they will likely be looking at you throughout their appointment. That means that your appearance is also an advertisement for your business. One of my physicians is a wonderful example of this. She wears brightly coloured shirts, bold jewelry and always has her hair and makeup done attractively. Her offices are neat and decorated in a unique fashion. It is enjoyable to go for my appointments with her.

You don't have to spend a lot of money to look and do your best - but you will likely earn more when you do!

SOUND - Confidentiality is a very important commitment you make to your clients. That means you need to ensure that the walls of your office are soundproof. If your client can hear sounds coming from outside of your private office, they immediately begin to think that others can hear them also.

Playing soft music can not only help to drown out any noises but also tends to help the client relax. I am cautious, however, that I do not play music with lyrics or songs that I know because I tend to start singing or humming. Also, I avoid classical music as it usually has strong variations in volume. One minute you are enjoying the quiet notes and then next - TA TA TA DAH!

Words are also very important and clients can become upset or shocked easily if things are said inappropriately or in the wrong tone of voice. Saying "That's right" is much better than "You told me that three times already".

SMELL - If we are in a room for an extended period of time we may not be aware of unpleasant smells. Perhaps I have recently heated up my lunch in the microwave and garlic fills the room. Maybe the couple's baby decided to fill his diaper during my last appointment. The smell of smoke which is on the clothing can remain strong for some time after the cigarette is extinguished.

Because of these issues, I always keep a couple of bottles of a light air freshener in my office. Whenever possible, I open the front door and invite nature to enter. There aren't many things that are better than the freshness provided by the great outdoors.

TASTE - Have you ever heard the expression "It gave me a bad taste in my mouth"? Sometimes a person who is upset or angry will use this saying to express his or her reaction to a situation.

I want my clients to leave with "a good taste in their mouth" and therefore always try to keep communication clear and open. Asking "Do I have that right?" and then listening to the response allows me to understand the person's perspective and, at the same time, lets them know that I do understand. I also encourage clients to be honest with me at all times and provide a non-judgmental environment so they know it is a "safe" thing to do.

Clients often feel thirsty during appointments. They may be on medications that dry their mouths or perhaps were exercising before they arrived. Low humidity in the room can also create thirst. Because of this, I have a small refrigerator in my meeting room and keep it filled with bottled water. I order cases of the water which is delivered with my office supplies so I don't need to carry it and the bottles can be recycled. No washing cups or glasses!

TOUCH - Many people have allergies or asthma so it is important to have a clean office without any materials that might be irritating to the skin or respiratory system.

I frequently am complimented by clients who expected a clinical setting and instead were welcomed into a comfortable and homey office. They state: "This feels like a sitting room" as I have love seats for seating, beautiful art and furniture of rich, dark wood.

Temperature is important for you and the client. A few months ago, our office was having serious problems with the heating system. We were roasting in the winter and could hang meat in the office during the hottest summer months! Many wrapped themselves in the colourful afghans that I had initially place in the office for decorative purposes.

I have found that when a client feels physically comfortable, he or she will want to return to that setting.

You do need to be very careful about if and when you physically touch anyone. Many people are threatened or uncomfortable if they are touched. Even shaking hands which was once a very acceptable practice is not welcomed by those who are concerned about spreading germs.

Try standing in the office doorway and pretending that you are entering the room for the first time. What are your five senses telling you about the tone of your business?

Leader or Manager?

Often the words leader and manager are used interchangeably and there has been debate about the differences between them. Generally speaking, however, leadership involves power through influence whereas management involves power by position.

In 1989 Dr. Warren Bennis, who is widely regarded as a pioneer of the contemporary field of Leadership Studies, drew distinctions between the two terms as follows:

- Managers administer, leaders innovate
- Managers ask how and when, leaders ask what and why
- Managers focus on systems, leaders focus on people
- Managers do things right, leaders do the right things
- Managers maintain, leaders develop
- Managers rely on control, leaders inspire trust
- Managers have a short-term perspective, leaders have a longer-term perspective
- Managers accept the status-quo, leaders challenge the status-quo
- Managers have an eye on the bottom line, leaders have an eye on the horizon
- Managers imitate, leaders originate
- Managers emulate the classic good soldier, leaders are their own person
- Managers copy, leaders show originality

I was raised in a family of entrepreneurs and therefore found it confusing to work in government agencies where focus was on the status-quo. Sometimes I was eager to start new projects or implement ideas but then faced disappointment because the manager did not see how these things would fit into the policies and procedures - even if they would have solved problems and expanded services.

I have also, however, been frustrated to work in businesses where the owner was a leader who hadn't developed policies and procedures to standardize administrative tasks. The result of this, of course, was that accounting and customer service always seemed to be in a mess!

Since I began operating my own business I have found that I have needed to be both leader and manager.

As the leader, I have laid out the vision and developed the business itself. This required an ability to innovate and independently take responsibility for not only starting my private practice but also for putting all of the pieces together in a way that it would operate at a profit.

At the same time, however, I have been manager. Ensuring that staffing, processes and administration are in place and then monitoring to ensure that tasks are completed in an orderly way are functions that are needed to maintain consistency and meet government and accounting standards.

One of the challenges of operating a private practice is to develop balance between your roles as both leader and manager. Being a professional requires that you not only learn to differentiate between them but also practice aspects of each so that you and your business will grow.

What hours will you work?

Setting your hours of work can be a challenging task! Your needs and the needs of your market will have to be considered and a plan established to ensure that they are met in the best way possible.

The Bible states "Man who does not work - does not eat". This also applies to women!

YOUR NEEDS:

1. Because you are a solo practitioner, your income depends on your ability to actually be working. That means that the first priority must be to protect your health. Individuals who work too many hours without having good self-care usually end up burning out and then cannot work. You therefore need to protect your health by balancing work and pleasure, eating a nutritious diet, exercising and getting enough rest. My grandpa used to say "If you have your health you can make your wealth".

2. Your financial needs will help to determine the number of hours that you will work. Start by determining the net annual income that you want. Then divide that number by the hourly fee you plan to charge. This will tell you the total number of hours that you will need to work in that year. Then divide this by 50 (allow two weeks for holidays) and you will know the number of hours that you will need to work each week. You will likely want to add a few more hours each week to allow for no shows, non-billable paperwork, statutory holidays or other circumstances that might interfere with or sabotage your plan.

3. One of the advantages of owning your own business is that you have some freedom to alter your work hours. A child's school concert, visiting relatives or participating in professional development opportunities can be benefits of private practice. Remember, however, that you will need to make up these hours when you are away from the office or your yearly goals will not be met.

4. There are always crises circumstances that cannot be predicted which will demand time away from the business. A broken water pipe, illness or other emergencies will affect your work hours.

Remember that every hour that you are away from the office means that you will not be earning income. Your absence also carries the risk of upsetting clients who were depending on you being there for their appointment time and disappointed clients might decide not to return in the future therefore costing you much more than the one hour session you missed.

YOUR CLIENTS' NEEDS:

1. Although our world has become much more flexible with work shifts and days off, there are some clients who will need to have early morning, evening or weekend appointments. You need to consider whether you want to set your office hours to accommodate these clients.

2. There are times that your clients will contact you and state that they cannot wait to see you until their next appointment. It is therefore important that you are able to assess the urgency of the situation, communicate with them by telephone to determine a suitable arrangement and possibly schedule an appointment beyond your regular work hours. Sometimes a short telephone conversation will help resolve a situation or assist the client until the date of their next appointment.

I suggest that people operate their businesses like jello that has set – be firm but flexible. Start your business with a set schedule in mind but be open to changing it based on specific needs of you or your client.

How big will you build?

Do you have an idea of how big you would like your business to be? Your answer will depend on the amount of time you wish to invest, the type of responsibilities you want to undertake and the reason that you had for starting the business.

My coworker, Richard, started a part-time psychology practice to pay for his two children's post-secondary education. I followed his example of part-time practice in addition to full-time employment in order to "test the waters" regarding whether I could move from my government job into my own private practice on a full-time basis.

One of my other peers uses his part-time practice fees to pay for a house in the mountains.

The type of business you will operate can range in size from one which provides a few extra dollars a month to a strong and financially strong operation with dozens of partners and employees.

There are several factors that will determine the size of business you will build:

1. **DESIRE** - People with different personalities have different ideas about how they would like to manage their work. Some have strong entrepreneur spirits and are happiest when they are putting together large conglomerates while others wish to remain independent and practice their craft without any partners or staff.

2. **FINANCIAL INVESTMENT** - If you are able to invest, finance or borrow money easily, you may be tempted to start your practice on a scale larger than those who begin on their own and expand when the money is available to do so.

Sometimes, forming a partnership allows those involved to develop a corporation or arrangement in which they can pool their money or secure larger start-up loans. You will need, however, to carefully consider the goals that each of you have. For example, how much income do you and your partners require from the company each month? What type of office do you want and how much will that cost? What the risk might be for everyone should one or more partners decides to leave the business in the future?

It is extremely important that you have a detailed Business Plan and a legal contract that clearly outlines the agreements that you have made with your partners before you start the business.

3. **TIME INVESTMENT** - I worked four hours in the first month of my business because I had a full-time position and was a little hesitant about leaving my salary and benefits. I didn't market or make specific efforts to increase my clientele beyond receiving unsolicited referrals.

In less than two years, I was so busy working in the evenings and on weekends that I decided to hire a Business Manager to help me decide if it was feasible to open a full-time private practice. My hourly fee was almost four times my government rate per hour and he convinced me that my pension and employee benefits could easily be replaced with private coverage. As I invested more and more of my time into the business and others became aware of the services I provided, it grew.

When you are creating your vision for the business, it is important to consider how big you want it to grow over time and what you are willing to do for that to happen.

Does your attitude reflect gratitude?

Often parents come to complain to me because their child has "an attitude"!

The dictionary defines attitude as a "state of mind or feeling".

Copyright 2001 by Randy Glasbergen. www.glasbergen.com

"That's our mission statement. If people follow that, everything else seems to fall into place."

We all have attitude! Some of us have an attitude that is defeatist while others positively believe anything is possible. Attitudes can affect self-esteem. Some people who feel unworthy of respect allow others to harm

25

them and settle for nothing while still others have narcissistic attitudes and state that they are so wonderful that they deserve everything!

Grief can be an attitude and so can celebration. In fact, over time, attitudes can change depending on one's circumstances, associates and experiences.

Recently, I was guest for a radio talk show where a caller asked why some people do well in life and others don't. My response was "We are the books we read, the people we spend time with and the things we listen to. If a person reads pornographic materials, hangs out with people who are negative or always in trouble and listens to music that promotes depression and death they are setting themselves up for problems."

Sarah Ban Breathnach, the author of *Simple Abundance*, recommends that each day you write down in a journal five things for which you are thankful. Once you have written something down, however, you cannot repeat that item again on another day. It is fairly easy to make the list for the first week or so but the task becomes much more demanding over time.

Try this exercise as it helps you think about your life from a different perspective. In fact, you will be challenged to think about the blessings in your life every single day.

Sometimes I believe it is effective to do just the opposite. Think about all the things that you don't have to deal with-like war, terminal illness, or malnutrition. Focusing on problems that you do not have to face can also help you to develop an attitude of gratitude.

Imagine that you have a piece of paper in one hand and a magnifying glass in the other. If you hold the glass on one spot, for an extended period of time, the paper will burn.

If the paper represents happiness and the glass represents your attitude it is therefore easy to see that having an attitude that views everything through a lens of trouble can eventually burn up your happiness. On the other hand, moving the glass around with an attitude of adventure and curiosity will prevent trouble and, at the same time, allow you to enjoy the world around you.

Attitude is a choice and each of us is responsible to cultivate and protect one that will promote health and happiness.

What influences you? Are the people you are around good examples? Are there people in your life who encourage you to grow? What can you do to improve your attitude?

You see, long-term business success begins with setting the vision and drawing your plan. If you do this with a positive attitude there is no limit as to what you can accomplish!

Planning Your Success

- ❑ Can you verbalize "why" you want a private practice?

- ❑ Have you assessed the risks of operating your business?

- ❑ Do you have a written vision?

- ❑ Have you drawn a blueprint for success?

- ❑ What will you name the business?

- ❑ Identify your areas of competency. How will you develop and maintain them?

- ❑ Who will be your ideal clients?

- ❑ Where will you locate?

- ❑ What tone do you want to set?

- ❑ How will you balance your roles as leader and as manager?

- ❑ What hours will you work?

- ❑ How big will you build?

- ❑ Do you have an attitude of gratitude?

Notes:

Chapter Two

UNDERTANDING VALUE AND MARKETNG YOUR PRACTICE

What do you value?

Define.com describes the term "values" as "beliefs of a person or social group in which they have an emotional investment (either for or against something)".

What values do you hold that you want to be evident in your business?

Let me share with you some of the ones that are important for a strong business:

Honesty - Truth is extremely important to me and it therefore guides all of my actions. I chuckle when I think about trying to return the "extra" twenty dollar bill that a client gave me in error some time ago. First of all the client was shocked that I wanted to return it. Then he stated that he didn't think it was his. Finally, he accepted the money with thanks.

It would have been easy for me to keep the money and not even mention it but I believe that honesty is a "black and white" issue.

A person is either honest in every aspect of life or they are dishonest.

When I say something and it doesn't come out right I try to immediately correct the statement. You see, even if it is a little uncomfortable, I believe it is better to clean it up right away.

When you are honest with other people, they will respect you and often will emulate your behaviours. And, better yet, you will likely sleep better knowing that there is nothing outstanding that might damage your reputation.

Excellence - "Good enough" is not "good enough". Strive to ensure that what you give to others is the best you can possibly give.

One of my goals is that every person will walk away from me stating "That was the best part of my day".

"My most valuable business skill? I know how to make you feel like the most important person in the whole world!"

It does not take much to be just a little better than your competitors and the clients appreciate that. Giving them a bottle of water, a handout or a compliment can lift their spirits and help them to feel comfortable. When your paperwork is error-free and your services are top-notch, both you and your client will feel satisfaction. Also, as my daughter says "When you build good relationships with clients, the money is the easy part".

Hope - Our clients usually come to us because they have a problem or want to avoid problems. They want to know that things can be resolved or prevented. Our job is to offer them the hope not only that things will be better but also that we can help them to become better.

United States President Obama did not have the experience or notoriety to help him win the election. In fact, he is the first to admit that it was highly unlikely for him to have been elected President. What he did offer the people, however, was exactly what they had been waiting for – a message of hope for the future. They wanted to vote for someone who would make improvements in their lives and solve problems they were facing. Barack Obama not only promised hope but also was a living example of the possibilities that dreams can come true for the least likely individuals through his personal story.

Finally, one of the important values that we can demonstrate and offer to family, friends and clients is a **spirit of adventure**. You see, when we approach life with the idea that we can take a few risks to gain amazing experiences, we will enjoy the journey in a new way. And when we encourage others to invite that spirit of adventure into their own lives, we have the added joy of watching them rekindle old dreams and approach new dreams with gusto.

Know the process

It doesn't matter what type of business you have, there are four basic steps in the process of serving clients. Once you understand and develop expertise with each of them, you will be able to not only please your existing clientele but also receive many referrals for new clients.

INTAKE - From the moment that you have your very first contact with an individual, your goal is to develop rapport. This involves building a trusting and comfortable relationship that will last over time. You will not only gather information from the client but also answer questions, schedule appointments and provide specific details that will help them to move further into the process.

Intake also involves explaining your business mandate - what you do offer as well as what you do not offer. If you feel that you cannot help the person, refer them to someone who can help.

Remember, you are building your reputation with every word and, even if the person decides not to use your products or services at this time, your contact may result in a sale or referral from them in the future.

ASSESSMENT - This is one of the most important things that you will do but one which is often neglected or done too quickly. It involves gathering enough information to understand the problems that the client is experiencing and how they might have tried to solve them in the past.

Ask good questions. When did the problem start? Were there any other things that occurred at the same time? Who else is involved? How are they affected? Knowing the "pain" that they are experiencing and the details of the situation are extremely important as you will then be able to provide the best solutions for resolving issues.

Assessment is an event and a process. You will need to do a good assessment of the problem at the beginning of your work with the client but also be asking questions and gathering information as the relationship progresses in order to provide other helpful suggestions.

INTERVENTION - This is the step where you show your expertise and offer appropriate recommendations to help the client with the problem. You will offer the client options and clearly explain the benefits and risks of each.

Interventions can be in the form of a product, training or even just a really good idea. They might involve referral to another professional or organization.

If you have done a thorough assessment and offer solutions that seem feasible, the client will know that you understand and therefore feel more trusting of you. The decision as to which, if any, of the options will be tried is always in the hands of the client but if the client is eager to resolve the issues and believes that you can help, s/he will be more likely to follow your recommendations.

How long does intervention take? It depends. Sometimes a client will find exactly what they needed in the first meeting with you. Others might take several weeks or months to become comfortable enough to fully open up about the problem, provide you with all the necessary information or gather confidence to try a recommendation. Still others might want a listening ear but never be able to do what is necessary to make positive change in their lives.

I have several clients who come to see me when they have an issue to discuss. We work on that, close the file, and then reopen it when they want to talk about something else.

One of my clients said "I believe that everyone should have a psychologist they can go to when they have difficulties". I agree with her. You see, life is not a smooth, straight highway. There are rumble bumps, curves and potholes for each person and it is therefore important that they have you to travel with throughout the entire trip.

EVALUATION – All of us need feedback and it is therefore important to check with the clients to find out how effective you were in meeting their needs.

Some clients may have disregarded everything you said and not followed through. Others may report a range of outcomes that resulted from your work with them.

Evaluation is similar to assessment in that it can be both an event and a process. You can get feedback by using simple questions such as "Is that correct?" or "Do you think this is a good suggestion?" and then make necessary adjustments immediately.

Some organizations provide the clients with written evaluation forms for them to complete during or after services have been provided. Others contact former clients to ask if and how the service was helpful for them.

No matter what method you use, it is very important to ask your clients for feedback. You might not like to hear what some of them have to say but it is better to know the truth and be able to improve than to have your business suffer while you are wondering why that is occurring.

I love the sign that I once saw in a hair salon. It read: "If you don't like our services – tell us - but if you like our services – tell everyone!"

That's a great policy that we, as business people, should all promote.

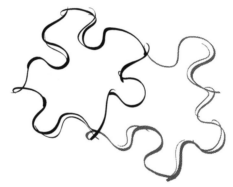

**VALUE IS WHEN YOU HELP THE CLIENTS
TO GET THEIR NEEDS MET
IN A HEALTHY WAY**

What is your specialization?

Therapists need to develop competency in a niche so that they can market in a very clear and targeted manner and provide the best services possible. A number of factors will help you to assess and define your niche.

1. **Your training and experience** - Competency refers to your ability to provide good, ethical services for your client. You develop this

through specific training and experience. Sometimes a psychologist decides to change or add to their competency and, in order to do this, needs to have a plan. It may include study, internship, supervision or a combination of these. How comfortable would you be if you were scheduled for brain surgery and found out that the person who would be operating was a pediatrician? Competency is a professional obligation and an ethical practice that results in confidence and expertise which both professional and client can value.

2. **Professional activities** – Therapists usually develop private practices that focus on Assessment, Treatment or a combination of these activities.

    Assessment - There are over 2000 psychometric tests which might be used in various combinations by those who are testing IQ, aptitude, personality, mental illnesses, or ability factors. Formal assessment usually involves conducting a clinical interview with the client, testing, obtaining collateral information and writing a full report with treatment recommendations.

    Treatment – Those who provide treatment services declare competency in one or more of clinical, counselling, educational, health, industrial, research or forensic fields of practice. The work usually involves having an initial intake appointment, review of reports and other information that is provided, setting appointments to establish goals with the client and introducing intervention options as well as ongoing assessment and referral for other services. There are numerous reasons for the treatment to end but the hope is that this occurs because the client has shown improvement.

    Other - There is also a wide range of other professional activities that therapists might participate in with roles as consultant, educator, author or speaker.

3. **Client Age** – You might choose to work with a specific population such as children and youth, adolescents, adults or seniors.

4. **Client Types** - A client may be one person who wants individual work, a couple, family, group, organization or community. You

will need to be careful that you know exactly who you client is in order to provide ethical service.

5. **Settings** - Most of your work will likely be completed in your own office, the office of another professional, a school, jail, hospital, or research lab but at times you might be quite surprised about where you will be required to provide services!

6. **Referral Sources** - Your practice may be one that takes referrals from a specific source or a combination that includes the Court system, Employee Assistance Programs, physicians, insurance companies, schools, or the general public.

The possibilities for developing your niche are almost unlimited. This allows you the opportunity to create a practice that will match your passion with the opportunities that available to you.

It is very important that you create a practice that will lead to day after day of wonderful work adventures so you will need to be thoughtful and clear about the work you will do.

Expanding your specialization

There are a number of ways that you can add to your knowledge, skills and abilities in order to expand the services which you will offer your clients. Following are five options which therapists might consider.

1. **Certified Substance Abuse Expert (C-SAE)** - Recognized training in assessment and treatment of addictions will help the therapist to understand issues and appropriate treatment options for the client.

2. **Certificate in Play Therapy -** There are a number of levels that can be completed when learning this area of practice. Of course, those who decide to practice play therapy will need to have an office setting that can accommodate this.

3. **Certificate in Hypnosis** - Many therapists use clinical hypnosis to help their clients deal with problems that they cannot otherwise remember or to help them relax enough to overcome specific difficulties such as migraines or anxiety.

4. **Professional Mediation certification** – Mediators help identify the things which clients can form agreement around to resolve their relationship, financial or parenting issues.

5. **Professional Speaking designation** - Frequently society is eager to have expert training or motivation from those who have worked as therapists. Speaking for various organizations can be in the form of workshops or keynote addresses.

There are thousands of ways that you can be creatively develop your business The popular motivational speaker, Zig Ziglar, says that to be successful we need to "find a need and fill it".

How do you assess value?

Sometimes businesses lose perspective when it comes to the product or service that they have to offer clients. Before you can do effective marketing, it is important that you are very clear about what you have to offer and whether it is helpful to your clients.

Think objectively about your products and services - Take some time to consider exactly what your client needs from their very first contact with you right through until their last contact. What was their first experience like? Were they treated in a friendly and respectful manner? Were they comfortable? Did they talk with you in an open and comfortable manner? What did you offer them? Did they take anything away with them after their first appointment? What are the trends that you hear over and over again? Is there a new product or service you could develop to help your clients?

Contact clients to get their opinions - It is important for you to ask what could have been improved. You are not on a mission to hear only positive comments. Ask them what product or services they could suggest that you offer in the future. Send them a written thank you for their input.

Research other private practices - Why re-invent the wheel? Most professionals are willing to share their ideas and would welcome your questions. In fact, they would likely be pleased and proud to show you the services, systems or products that they have developed. You might even ask them to critique an area of your business that you feel could be improved.

Record your findings - Documenting what you have learned does not have to be complex. In fact, three pages would capture everything in an organized manner. On one sheet of paper write "Business strengths". On another write "Things to improve or develop" and on a third page write "Action steps required".

Assessing your business requires an openness to hear the truth and a willingness to change or create the things that will better serve the clients.

Are you a good listener?

Adding value for your clients

Often clients will return over and over again while also referring others because they believe they receive good value in the services you offer. A little planning and the use of automation can assist every professional in achieving and maintaining value.

Following are a number of ways in which you can go "above and beyond" what other businesses are offering.

1. **Provide appropriate referrals** - When a client asks for a product or service that I do not offer, I give them the contact information for the person or organization who would likely best meet their needs. Frequently, the client has been unaware of free or low-cost resources that I suggested.

When regular clients require a referral letter to another professional, I prepare and send it without cost. Also, if I have a business card or brochure for that professional, I give it to the client.

2. **Prepare handouts** - Whenever I find that I am repeating the same information over and over again, I prepare an appropriate handout which I can give to the clients. For example, "My Favourite Authors" lists experts with various specialties. This handout allows me to circle the name of author who I believe would be best suited for the client and provides space for me to write the name(s) of particular books that the client can access through a library or bookstore.

3. **Offer to have other family members attend sessions with the client** - Sometimes a client is more comfortable by having someone attend appointments to help them answer questions, share pertinent information or provide support for them. Over the years, I have found that allowing this also helps with understanding and follow through as the person who accompanies the client can help to encourage the client between appointments.

4. **Respond to crisis calls quickly** – You must be careful not to allow your client's crisis to become your crisis, however, responding to a client's call quickly can often alleviate an even bigger crisis. A few minutes of conversation by telephone should focus on helping the person to relax, putting things in proper perspective and setting up some action steps to deal with the issue at hand. Doing this helps to build trust. At the next session, however, make it a priority to set boundaries and develop a plan for the client to use in the event that another crisis occurs between appointments. This may involve specific strategies or sharing information about crisis services in the community.

5. **Provide bonus items or services -** A bottle of cold water on a hot day, colourful stickers for children or calling a taxi can be ways of adding value. Some businesses have a popcorn machine in the waiting room. A dentist may offer the patient

a new toothbrush after an appointment. Other professionals might help to educate the client with a brochure, audio product, handout or book.

Providing value-added service does not usually cost you more than time and creativity but it can make a big difference to your bottom line. You see, operating a successful business requires developing good relationships that will last over time.

Satisfied clients who receive good value will return to you when they need help and also recommend that their friends and family contact you. When this happens, everyone wins!

The value of referrals

REFERRALS

In order to have a strong, active and growing business, you will need to have good referral sources and also be able to provide appropriate referrals for your clients to receive services that you do not offer. Building and nurturing relationships with others will result in a steady stream of new clients for your practice.

Referral sources

There are many different types of referral sources that can be cultivated as follows:

1. **Word of Mouth** - For years, marketers have stressed the fact that the best form of advertising is by individuals who talk about your services in a positive manner. Former clients as well as their friends and relatives can personally attest to the satisfaction they

gained by working with you and will likely begin referring their acquaintances for assessment and/or treatment. It doesn't take long until a community forms an opinion about you and your private practice. I remember hearing the words of a lawyer a few years ago who stated "It takes a lifetime to build a reputation and only a few seconds to lose it". What you do and how you do it will help to determine the future success of your business.

2. **Other Professionals** - At times you might set up joint ventures so that the client can benefit from having different types of services provided by a number of professionals. In a divorce situation, for example, a lawyer, psychologist and accountant may all offer their unique expertise as they work together to help the client through the process.

    Other professionals may ask you to provide a service for their clients. For years, for example, I have been completing psychological assessments for an infertility specialist. He claims that he does not have ethical practice unless the individual or couple has had this assessment done before he begins treatment.

    Referral sources come in a variety of forms. You may receive referrals from teachers who ask you treat their students, managers who are concerned about their employees or other professionals in your community who trust you to help meet the client needs.

3. **Government and Public Service Agencies** - The Justice system, community service organizations and government departments might refer individuals to you for either assessment or treatment services. Some such as the *Workers' Compensation Board* or *Health Canada* might actually pay for the clients but usually this is based on a fixed fee schedule that they have set. There are times when your contract will allow you to ask the client to "top up" the fees if the organization's scale is lower than your rate. If this is not allowed, however, you will need to decide whether you are willing to work for their lower fee but, in exchange, receive a steady stream of referrals from that source.

4. **Employee Assistance Programs (EAPs)** - Some companies offer their employees a benefit plan with a limited number of sessions or a set yearly amount to cover their therapy fees. Most allow dependents and/or eligible family members to also receive these services. The benefits are available to the employee on a yearly basis and cannot be carried over into the following year so it's a situation of "use it or lose it". Some employees also are given a "Health Spending Account" which is a set amount that they can choose to use each year for a number of defined services such as medications, dental work or therapy.

    Most of these programs require that the therapist sign a contract with the EAP company for the fee per hour that they are willing to pay and agree to comply with their company policies.

5. **Private Benefit Plans** - Some people purchase coverage for themselves and their family members to ensure that they can obtain health services if and when they are needed. In Alberta, for example, there are different levels and options for those who want to purchase plans through *Blue Cross*. The premiums and benefits vary according to the plan that the individual chooses.

6. **Insurance Company Plans** - Companies like *Manulife*, *Cooperators* and *Great West Life* offer a variety of types of coverage for their policy holders. Some plans have a limited amount per year to cover therapy sessions. Others offer short-term and long-term coverage for those who are unable to work due to disability. Usually, if the client is working, s/he is required to pay the fee and then submit receipts to the insurance company for reimbursement. Sometimes, however, an employee or "worker" from the insurance company will negotiate a fee with the therapist for a limited number of sessions and then pay the therapist directly for these on behalf of the client who is on a medical leave from the workplace.

7. **Professional Referral Services -** Some professional organizations charge their members a yearly fee for referral services. Individuals from the public who contact the organization and request the contact information for competent therapists are then referred to the members who have subscribed to this service.

Newsletters and magazines published by professional organizations also usually offer advertising options which can be purchased by members.

8. **Self-referrals** - I frequently receive telephone calls or emails from individuals who have found me in the yellow pages, through Internet searches or one of my newspaper columns.

Offer excellent service, maintain a respectable reputation and develop good relationships with referral sources and you will soon enjoy having not only a strong client base but also a steady stream of new business.

Preparing referrals

There are times that you will not be able to help your clients and when this occurs it is important that you refer them to appropriate services that can and will assist them. There are six things need to be considered when making referrals.

1. **Client Needs** - In order to accurately prepare an appropriate referral, you will need to do an assessment. Gather information about the client and ask him/her what they feel would be helpful. Your expertise is important as clients often do not know what they need or think that you are the "answer" to their problems. There are also times when you will need to be wise in deciding which problems need to be dealt with first in order to relieve stress for the client.

2. **Service Options** - Understanding the types of services that are available will help you to explain them to the client. Knowing the mandate, strengths and weaknesses of the organization or professional will help the client make a good choice about who to see. I find that my clients greatly appreciate both my knowledge and honesty when it comes to helping them find a suitable specialist or program.

3. **Consent** - Before you make any contact with the office or organization where you are referring the client, ensure that you have full informed consent from the client. This is best done in written format.

4. **Transition** - I usually talk with the client about how I will complete the referral and explain how much information will be sent in the referral letter. I also ensure that they know the address, contact information, and approximate timeframe in which they will be seen by the other professional. Asking the client to contact me if they have not been contacted regarding an appointment time shows them that I am concerned that they do receive the appropriate services in a timely manner.

5. **Follow up** - At the client's next appointment with me, I read the referral letter to them so they know what was said about them. I also gather information from them about the experience they had in booking an appointment. If they have already had their appointment, I ask them to tell me about it and whether they felt it was helpful for them. If I have received any reports from the professional, I review them with the client and we discuss how any recommendations that were made might be implemented into our treatment plan.

6. **Building the Referral Network -** When clients have been pleased with the referred services, I continue to work with that office.

Exchanging business cards, brochures or other information will not only help the clients but also strengthen the relationship and ultimately result in further referrals back and forth between you and the other agency.

Sometimes it takes time for referrals to come your way. Do not panic. This might be because there is another therapist who has been working with that office for a significant period of time. Loyalty is usually strong, especially if a relationship has been built and maintained over the years.

If you are wondering how you can improve the relationship with a referral source, remember that most people love to be taken out for lunch! Ask good questions about how you can enhance your relationship and ultimately receive referrals from that person. Then follow the advice that you have been given.

Be patient. Building relationships takes time!

We are not all things to all people and therefore need to ensure that we can make appropriate referrals so client needs will be met. And doing this is all part of the wonderful adventure that is known as building a business.

Your fee schedule

Those who are starting a new business might have difficulties setting the fee schedule that they will use for their clients. There are several factors that will help to determine the appropriate rates:

1. **Your local market** - You will need to do some research for your community or area. The cost of living and number of services available all affect the demand for the services that you provide. Not everyone will be able to afford what you offer and it is therefore important that you know the free public or low-fee services which you can recommend through referrals.

2. **Your competition** - There may be other professionals who at first glance appear to offer similar services to yours. Those who state that they provide "counselling", for example, can differ greatly in their training, professional designation and experience. You need to consider this as well as the comparative effectiveness of your services. Many people who state that they are "therapists" may not get good results or not be considered by the clients as being "helpful".

   You are unique – as a person and as a professional. Remember this and have confidence!

3. **Your self-image** - I was a Social Worker before I trained as a psychologist and therefore had been used to working in the public sector. I found it difficult at that time to go from $34.00 per hour salary to $140.00 per hour fee that was recommended, at the time, by my professional organization.

   I had studied for a number of years and invested a great deal of effort into my preparation for private practice. I guess I just hadn't mentally grown into the professional role yet.

My Business Manager asked me a number of questions about what I had to offer the clients and we agreed that I had the required expertise so would set the $140.00 rate for the next three clients. They all accepted this without question.

Since then, I have become more comfortable in charging an appropriate professional fee that recognizes the value I provide.

At times, I have wondered if people would be willing to pay my fees if I increased them. My concerns were always unfounded and, in fact, I was quite surprised to learn that some people believe that the more they pay for something, the higher the quality they will receive. They actually choose the services that they will hire based on the price – and the higher the price the more they want it!

Consider using the "sleep factor". What fee will you charge that allows you to sleep at night? It must be one that pays your bills and gives you a feeling that what you offer is worth the hourly fee.

4. **Your colleagues (the fees of other professionals with whom you collaborate)** - One day a while ago, my son asked me "How many years of education does the lawyer who is upstairs in your building have and what is her fee per hour?" My answer was "She has a four year degree and charges $350.00 per hour". He then asked the same questions about me and I replied "I have eleven and a half years of education, the same number of years of experience and charge $160.00 per hour".

The lawyer and I were working with the same clients at the time and I was providing good value for them at less than half the fee!

You need to look around the community and determine your value in comparison to other professionals. (And you need to listen to the questions that your children ask you).

5. **Your financial goals and needs** - Calculate all of the expenses required to operate your business. Divide that by the amount you plan to charge for a billable hour in order to determine the number of hours you will need to work each month to pay

the bills. Then determine the amount that you would like as a personal income and divide that by your expected hourly fee. Now you will know the number of billable hours that you will need to work in order to meet your financial goals.

You may need to adjust the hourly fee or the number of hours to accomplish what you plan to do. (And don't forget that there are activities in every business that are required but not billable so make sure you are working enough "billable" hours to meet your goals).

6. **Your professional organization** - A recommended fee schedule usually states the hourly fee that a newly-registered professional can use. You will need to adjust this based on the above factors and the specific expertise that you offer.

7. **Your contracts** - Determining your fee schedule can be a difficult task that requires both thought and flexibility. If you are approached to sign a contract with an insurance company or employee benefit plan you will likely be offered a lower rate and may choose to take it in exchange for a steady stream of referrals from them. Remember though, that a lower fee means that you will be working more hours in order to meet your financial goals.

8. **The amount of risk involved** – One of my friends who is a psychologist explained to me that we get paid well because of the amount of risk involved in the work we do. It is not uncommon for therapists to be reported by disgruntled clients and the costs for a liability situation can be huge.

There are also specific roles and activities that led to significant emotional stress. For example, completing a custody assessment for the Court system can be much more professionally and personally demanding than talking with a student about career goals. The type of work you plan to do will therefore play a large part in determining the fee you will charge. Higher risk – higher fee.

9. **Client options** - People choose to have their needs met in different ways and some will not want to pay the fee you have set no matter what it might be. Others may be limited by the benefits they are

allowed. Whether it is because of economic status or personal preference, society does provide different options to accommodate this and you should not feel badly if a potential client chooses a service other than yours because of the price.

Just consider the fact that some people pay hundreds of dollars to have their hair styled. Others shop for bargain services and still others do the cut themselves! It's all about personal choice.

In my practice I do not usually offer pro bono (free) services. Instead, I do good referrals to other quality services for those who cannot afford my fees. I also ensure that I use a share of all my profits for philanthropic purposes so that many are helped through my giving rather than just a few.

Advertising and publicity

Once you have a clear idea of the services you will offer and the clientele you will serve you will need to consider how you will market and promote your business.

There are many differences between advertising and publicity, not the least of which is the cost associated with each. You may decide to do some paid advertising but you will also need to develop a public relations plan that will promote your services without draining your time or financial resources.

Traditionally, businesses have been used to paying media sources to advertise their products or services through commercials on television and radio or in printed forms published in newspapers and magazines. In fact, some large businesses hire public relations organizations whose focus is to find ways to convince consumers to "buy" through strategic planning.

Bill Stoller, a professional publicist who has created a website for "Savvy businesses and Entrepreneurs" entitled *Publicity Insider* describes publicity as "the simple act of making a suggestion to a journalist that leads to the inclusion of a company or product in a story".

Now unless you have some experience as a publicist, you might feel slightly overwhelmed. The truth is that all forms of media have a large amount of space and time to fill in order to educate and entertain their readers and listeners. They need your story. You just need to know how to bridge the gap between what the media wants and what you have to offer.

When I was in high school, I wrote a weekly column for our small town newspaper and enjoyed the experience. Approximately three years ago I was asked to promote *Psychology Month* in Alberta. Because I had done some work with the media for a charity function I thought it might be a good idea to offer to do a column which I pitched as "All Psyched Up". Our city's newspaper liked the idea and I have been writing weekly for five years!

A few months later, a lady from my home town read a couple of the submitted articles and took them to the editor of my hometown newspaper. So, I am now writing a column in the same little newspaper where I was featured thirty-five years ago! As an adolescent I was paid by the inch so my articles were loooong. Now I submit my column without being paid despite having earned four university degrees! I laugh when I tell others that it just goes to show that education doesn't always pay big rewards!

That column in two newspapers has opened so many doors for me.

Often we receive calls from readers who want to schedule appointments to work on psychological problems they have been experiencing. We have sold more of my first book because of my writing than might otherwise have sold. In fact, one of the newspaper editors purchased twenty books to give to staff for Christmas gifts.

I am now also a "media consultant" in the community and am called to help journalists write on diverse topics that I would never have considered such as "What is the psychological effect of having a pet?" or "How do people view Friday the thirteenth?"

A few years ago, there was a triple murder in Medicine Hat. I was asked to be a guest on two one-hour radio talk shows. The Country station who hosted this was shocked and unprepared when the phone lights were jammed. Radio, television and newspapers contacted me for interviews as the trial progressed. In fact, a friend called from Vancouver to excitedly explain that she had just seen me on the evening news report.

And it all started with one article!

You don't have to be a writer, though, in order to receive free but invaluable media coverage. Those who do charity work are often chased for interviews and photos. In fact, anything that might capture the interest of the public is likely something that could be picked up by the media. You just need to learn how to "pitch" it.

Last fall I registered for the *On Air Publicity* course talk by British Columbia's morning man, Wayne Kelly. His training is focused on learning how to present yourself in a professional but unique manner to get the attention of the media. I learned so much that will help me for the rest of my career - not just in gaining free publicity but also in understanding how the interesting world of the media works and what to do when they approach me.

25 no cost ways to promote

P.T. Barnum used creativity and imagination to attract people to the *Big Top* circus and other unusual sideshows. He is renowned for the marketing example he set for others and his statement "Without promotion something terrible happens - nothing!"

We are often limited by the amount of money they can invest in advertising and even if you do have a large budget, that doesn't mean you should spend it without careful planning.

There are many ways that you can promote your services with little or no cost.

Following are 25 ideas for you to consider:

1. Offer excellent service and encourage your clients to send you referrals

2. Write a column or articles for your newspaper

3. Sit on a community board or committee and network with the others who are involved

4. Do volunteer work in a charitable organization

5. Teach a class at a College or University (you will likely be paid for this and promote your business at the same time)

6. Offer to give speech for an organization

7. Open a Facebook and LinkedIn account with your business profile

8. Make an appointment to meet with a journalist in the community and offer to be their consultant

9. Teach a workshop for an employment agency or high school class

10. Prepare a Media Release and send it to radio, television and newspapers (remember: technology allows you to be international right from home)

11. Mentor a new immigrant

12. Write a newsletter and distribute it by email to clients and media

13. Give discount certificates for charity auctions

14. Become an active participant in your professional association

15. Sign up for a free Twitter account and learn how to build relationships with it

16. Meet other professionals and exchange referrals with them

17. Put brochures or handouts in the *Welcome Wagon* baskets

18. Host your own Internet radio show

19. Become involved in campaigns to clean up the neighbourhood

20. Start a blog with a free account at *Wordpress.com*

21. Put your business cards or a poster with tear-off strips on community bulletin boards

22. Be a guest on a radio or television show

23. Offer to promote your profession during their yearly campaign

24. Write articles and submit them to Internet directories

25. Introduce yourself to people every day!

Learn about enticing and attracting others to you and your business through creativity. The key to promotion is to build relationships with others.

Telephone directory advertising

Solo practitioners do not usually have full-time staff to serve receptionist duties during open hours. There are several ways that you can use the telephone to promote your business even without staff. One of these is to carefully consider the way that you promote your business in telephone directories.

The costs for listing your telephone number in a telephone book can be shocking and it is therefore important that you know your choices and make purchasing decisions wisely.

There are three basic types of telephone listings - white pages, yellow pages and Internet yellow pages.

Before you agree to any telephone directory advertising begin by studying your telephone book. Notice the things that draw your eye and attention to specific listings. In the white pages, I have paid extra, for example, to have my business name and number highlighted in yellow. This not only grabs the reader's attention but also helps them to be able to focus on the number while dialing

Yellow page ads vary by category, size and colour. Some include graphics, pictures or symbols. I found that costs for even more than a couple of lines in the yellow pages were more than I wanted to pay.

Resolving this was easy. First of all, I chose an advertising package which allowed me to place two lines in each of three separate categories in the yellow pages. On the first line of my listing I state my business name, credentials, address and telephone number. On the second line is my website address. I paid extra to have my name highlighted in blue so it stands out in each category.

Clients have told me that when they are searching for a psychologist they turn to the yellow pages and usually begin calling each number from the top of the list downwards. They leave voice mail messages and while they are waiting for their message to be returned they check out my website. This allows them to start developing a personal connection with me. They can read my bio and background history, view a map which shows them the location of the office and consider the types of services that I provide.

Within minutes, I usually receive a second message requesting an appointment!

This year, I was contacted by the company that owns *Yellow Pages* online and a proposal was made for me to have a video on their site. After careful consideration I decided that there were other places where the advertising dollars would likely benefit me more. You see, many of my clients do not have computer access or would turn to a printed directory before going online. You will need to think about the people who would be looking for your services and make a decision with that in mind.

Promotion using this technique not only saves me a great deal of money, but also allows the client to have an opportunity to learn far more about my business than an advertisement would provide. The added bonus, of course, is that I have control over my website and can make changes whenever they are needed. You can't do that with a printed directory or an Internet directory that is owned by another company.

Use the telephone directory in a way that can help the public to begin the wonderful adventure of being involved with you and your business!

5 free online tools for marketing

Many solo professionals expect that merely opening the door in the morning will fill the bank account. Not true!

The whole idea of marketing is to draw attention to yourself and your business and then show the prospect how you or your services can help them solve their problems. They will likely not be willing to use your services, however, until they know, like and trust you.

The Internet is a tool that can facilitate the relationship but many people are skeptical or concerned that they will be scammed.
You need to let the world know that you are ready and willing to meet their needs and that you can be trusted.

There are many online tools that are low or no-cost which can help you to do that.

Following are five "no" or "low" cost internet tools which can be used to extend your marketing reach. Each allows you to prepare a profile. You will need to do this with a great deal of thought but once you have the profile properly completed, you will merely update it if and when things change.

Blog - There are many different types of blogs and some, such as WordPress.com, are free. These allow you to not only set up a profile that represents your products and services, but also allows you to post information through text, audio or video on a regular basis. This keeps the attention of the reader who will return often to see what is "new".

Linked In - This is a site that is focused primarily on business and business people. Again, you will develop a profile but this time it is with the hope that you will capture the attention of employers, employees or people who are interested in setting up joint ventures with you.

Facebook - Although some people use this only as a way to personally connect with friends and family, you can also develop a business site and invite others to be your Friend or Fan. Facebook also offers you the opportunity to announce an "Event" to those who are in your groups and invite them to live or teleseminar sessions that you have planned.

MySpace - I used to have a business page on this site but found that many people who use *MySpace* are only interested in developing personal or romantic relationships. Even showing clearly in your profile that you are there for business purposes might not dissuade those who have other goals. It is still a good idea to have a business profile on this site as long as you are aware of the goals of others and have a plan regarding how you might handle their non-business contacts.

Twitter - One of the newest forms of social networking is through this method. Once again, you begin by signing up for a free account and preparing a profile. You are then encouraged to "follow" people who you think are interesting and can even follow those who are following them. Most will politely follow you back. You communicate with those who are connected through messages that must be no longer than 140 characters. Relationships are built as you share information and learn about others.

There are many, many others forms of social media which can be used to promote your services and build strong connections with others. The danger in becoming involved in social media, however, is that time can slip away quickly and you might neglect other aspects of building your business. It is therefore important to set out a schedule which will help you to manage your time and then strictly follow it.

Internet and social networking is just one more way that you can turn your business into a wonderful adventure through relationship building.

Your website and blog

Solo professionals can greatly enhance their private practice by developing a website or blog. Of course, the first advantage to doing this is that it forces you to be very clear about who you are, what you offer and how you are going to present that to the Internet world.

Although both are designed to present you in the best possible manner, there are several differences between a website and blog as follows:

Your website - Most professionals either don't have the skills or the time to design and develop a website so you will likely need to hire a web designer to do this. Websites can be developed for a few hundred dollars or a few thousand dollars - depending on what you want and the hours required to accomplish this

You will probably be paying for the work by the hour or on a contracted rate based on the number of pages you will have at your website. The more thought and planning you have done before meeting with the designer, the more money you will save.

Do your research. Begin by looking at some of the websites of professionals in your field. Notice the colours, font, pictures and information that are displayed and write down what you like and don't like about them. Make sure you have the website addresses recorded so that you will be able to show them to the designer as examples of your preferences.

Search for a web designer that will meet your needs. The least expensive is not always the best match for you. Ask to see samples of their work and ensure that you have a firm quotation before starting so you are not surprised by the costs. Also ask for references from others who have worked with the designer. You might also ask for a meeting to assess whether you feel that the designer is suitable - but you will likely need to pay for the time involved with this.

If you don't have an idea of what you want, it will be hard to obtain an accurate quote. Begin making your plan for what you want the website to look like and what it will promote for you. Briefly sketch out a list of the topics that you would like to cover on the website, the number of pictures you want to use and the approximate number of pages required.

It is important to note that a website will need to be updated by your web designer. You therefore will want to consider the "life" of the site as information or pictures that are outdated will result in added costs.

You do not have much control of the website after it is prepared and will be paying more in the future to change it.

Your blog - If you are interested in having more control over the information that you will be putting on the Internet, you might consider buying a domain, setting up hosting and then designing a blog.

Many professionals are choosing a blog over a website because they can set it up themselves with very little training and update it on a regular basis. In fact, blogs allow you the opportunity to post messages or articles several times a day if you wish.

I like using blogs for posting articles that I have written for my newspaper columns. This allows me the option of sorting them into categories and also allows the viewer to type a specific word into the search box to find relevant information.

Blogs also have a statistical function which tells you the number of views you have had each day as well as the most viewed posts. This helps you to assess and understand the needs of the market.

A blog with domain name and hosting can be set up for less than one hundred dollars (and your time investment).

I have several websites and blogs. One of my websites is designed to serve my psychology contracts and clients. Another is for my speaking and writing business. One is for the time I am with grandchildren. I am also developing a new blog which will chronicle my trips and adventures.

The Internet offers several opportunities for you to promote your services but the hub for any business is a website, a blog or both.

Consider your budget and the amount of time that you have available to begin developing your Internet presence. The answer to these questions will help you to choose whether you will learn how to build a blog or hire a web designer to assist you. Or perhaps you might decide to hire a web designer to build your blog and then train you to do the updates.

30 things to consider for your website

If you are planning to develop a website for your business there are at least thirty things to consider before you even contact a web designer:

1. Colour - Besides considering your favourite colour, you might want to do research about the psychological effects that colour has on individuals. The colour you choose will likely be used on other marketing materials, forms and products in order to brand your business so choose something that you will be proud of long-term.

2. Logo or Business Symbols - These will be part of your branding and used in all of your marketing materials so make sure you have a good design that you like.

3. Business name - Ensure that there is consistency in how you display your name on everything. Use identical wording, punctuation and font. (If you are planning to incorporate your business, secure your business name before beginning the marketing).

4. Business address - You might want to have a map beside the address to help the client find your office. Put all contact details including the postal or zip code for those who will be mailing cheques and other information to you.

5. Telephone numbers - Include the area code for all numbers. (It is a time saver and easier to just give one number that has voice mail and then check it often rather than having two or more numbers).

6. Other websites or blog addresses - You might want to use the symbol or an icon for other sites such as the "F" widget for Facebook. Each site usually has an application that allows you to put a symbol on your site. When viewers click on the symbol they are taken directly to the other location.

7. Your Photo - This allows the client to see you and form a connection before you even meet each other. Ensure that you are smiling and look friendly! Put your name and academic designations under the picture to show your credibility and allow the client to connect you with your expertise.

8. A Biography - Viewers will appreciate being able to read a short but comprehensive biography that outlines your background and credentials.

9. Your Education - Include all of your academic and workshop achievements.

10. Your Experience - You can use bullets or a point-form style but do include everything that will help the viewer to know you better.

11. Affiliations - This listing will include organizations where you have served or where you hold a current membership. Affiliations usually reflect your values.

12. Publications - These are the articles, projects or products that you have completed and will again help to demonstrate your expertise in specific areas.

13. Services Offered - Be very clear about the types of services which you offer such as assessment, treatment, mediation or hypnosis.

14. Speaking and/or Training - Outline topics which you are prepared to present or describe topics you have offered in the past.

15. Links - You may want to set up a listing of professional organizations or websites that offer important information for the viewer.

16. Achievements - Perhaps you would like to add a page for specific awards or experiences of which you are proud.

17. Referral Information - State the types of referrals you accept and give directions regarding how they should be prepared and communicated to you.

18. Fee Schedule – Either list your fees or set up a link to another site which you can update.

19. Insurance or EAP payments - Provide instructions for accessing programs that will help to pay fees.

20. Policies - Outline the way that appointments will be booked, the length of the sessions and the way that non-attendance with be handled.

21. Contact information - Offer an email address for those who prefer computer over telephone.

22. Articles or links to articles on specific topics.

23. Product Page – Include this if you have items for sale. Photos and/or videos enhance this page as well as clear descriptions of the products.

24. Audio links or downloads of information or recorded training sessions

25. Video clips which can serve several purposes such as welcoming visitors to the website, educating them or developing rapport.

26. Media Page - Include a Media Release, listing of radio, newspaper or television interviews completed and possibly links which would facilitate reading or listening to them.

27. Any pertinent forms that can be downloaded and completed by the client.

28. Photos to enhance your credibility or promote your services. For example, a picture of your office building might help the new client to find you more easily. You might also include high resolution photos which media could use in articles about you.

29. A calendar showing your schedule or open business days.

30. Unsolicited testimonials from individuals who praise or promote your services.

Remember, the more work that this entails for the designer, the more it will cost you. You might pay by the hour, the number of pages on the site or by a contracted rate. Whatever you do, make sure that you are clear about what you want as this will save you both time and money!

10 things to know about the media

Often solo professionals are contacted by radio, television, newspapers or magazines and asked to contribute to the "story" they are working on. It is very important that you understand what you are doing so you will not say things you will regret but instead will benefit from the promotion and help the audience. Following are some basic facts that will get you started on the right foot.

1. **Goals** - The media want to educate and entertain their audience. To do this they try to draw the attention of the audience, get the "scoop" and sell themselves to the world. Your goals may not mesh with their goals so you will have to be clear about whether you will participate when you are called and how you will contribute.

2. **Timelines** - Most times, journalists and reporters are on a very short timeline and need to have your interview or information immediately. You do not have to respond or participate - especially if you do not have time to think about what you will say.

3. **Competency** - Media personnel are not trained about your area of expertise and therefore may ask you about things out of your competency. This is your opportunity to educate them and do appropriate referrals.

4. **Boundaries** - One of the slogans for media is "What bleeds - leads". Another is "sex sells". You might be asked questions that seem to pressure you to say things that are inaccurate, confusing or misleading. Don't get trapped. Think about the question and your answer very carefully.

5. **Clarity** - Ensure that you immediately correct any errors that the media make. It is better to explain things to the journalist or reporter while you are on air or during the interview than to try to correct the mistakes after they are aired or in print.

6. **Honesty** - If you don't know - say you don't know. If you don't have information that has been requested, be clear about the fact that you don't have the information. Just tell the truth in a simple manner.

7. **Confidentiality** - There are many things that are not acceptable to share with the media. Be very cautious! Even if you don't use names, some people might think you are talking about them (or their friends) based on the details you provide. Saying too much will not only hurt your client but may actually destroy your reputation and business.

8. **Speculation** - If you haven't seen a person professionally, you cannot comment on their condition. (If you have seen them, you cannot comment because of confidentiality). You will therefore need to stick to answering questions using research or general patterns rather than specifics. Be careful! Don't get trapped into saying something you didn't mean to say!

9. **Your Professional Profile** - Prepare and gather together information that the media can use repeatedly. I have a website and blog with pages designed for the media. They include my bio, high resolution pictures, a Media Release and Media Page. They also include my past media involvement and a listing of the speaking engagements that I have done over the past three years. When you set up a site, the journalist or reporter has access to the information needed to support your expertise - and having everything on a website saves you a great deal of time!

10. **Preparation** - The media is not interested in everything you have to say about a topic. In fact, they tend to focus on "sound bites" or "quotes" and it is therefore important that you offer them good information in the proper format. Consider the questions that might be asked and write down carefully worded answers. Practice explaining things in short, complete sentences. If you have advance notice of the topic, quickly write down the points that you want to cover during the interview before it begins.

Working with the media can be a rich and rewarding aspect of your business - or a nightmare - depending on how you answer the questions and how your information is used. But even when you do everything "right" there can still be misquotes, errors or even things that you said which are taken out of context.

Just like any aspect of your business, building relationships with the media takes time and respect.

If you are planning to work with the media as part of your business building strategy, you will likely want to study and prepare for this with an expert in the field. Wayne Kelly at www.onairpublicity.com will help you to understand the system and develop your media savvy so that everyone will benefit when you are called for that interview!

Planning Your Success

❑ Can you name your work values?

❑ Do you know the four steps of the process for helping people?

❑ What is your specialization?

❑ How can you expand your specialization?

❑ How can you assess and add value for your clients?

❑ Who are the professionals who will send and receive referrals?

❑ Have you set up a fee schedule?

❑ Do you understand the difference between advertising and publicity?

❑ Are you familiar with the 25 no cost ways to promote?

❑ Have you developed a plan to save on telephone directory advertising?

❑ Do you know the 5 free online tools for marketing?

❑ Have you created a website and blog for your business?

❑ Do you know the 30 things to consider for your website?

❑ Have you studied the 10 most important things about dealing with the media?

Notes:

Chapter Three

CREATING A WONDERFUL ENVIRONMENT

Rent, lease or own

There are several options when it comes to deciding where you will operate your business and provide services for your client, each with advantages and disadvantages. It is therefore important that you seriously consider which option is best for the time being.

Rent - When I first started seeing clients, I paid an hourly rate to a psychiatrist for one room in his office. This allowed me freedom as I did not have to be committed to all the expenses associated with operating an office but still had the opportunity to use a professional space when needed. I had my administration office in my home and would do my paperwork there but never take a client into my residence. This situation also allowed me to use a portion of my home costs as income tax write offs.

You might want to rent office space on an hourly, daily, weekly or monthly basis. Sometimes space is furnished and other times, you will need to set up the room or rooms with your own furnishings. Remember to consider the extra costs you will incur if you are required to purchase items.

Lease - Often businesses or individuals who are renting out office space want a commitment and may ask that you sign a lease which will outline the expectations and conditions they have for you to fulfill. Read this very carefully. You may consider having a lawyer review it before signing. You may be able to negotiate a lower rent by offering to sign for longer periods of time. When I moved into my present location in a professional building, the space was in dire need of renovations. The building representatives and I agreed to share the costs of this and then the owners made an offer to lower the monthly rent in exchange for a three year commitment rather than the two-year commitment that I had proposed. I gladly signed.

The disadvantages of a lease, of course, are that you are locked in for a set period of time and, if you decide to move before the lease expires, are responsible for paying the full amount owing to the expiry date. The advantage of a lease is that you are guaranteed an office so can prepare all of your marketing materials with that in mind. Being locked in, however, can be motivating for you. You know that you must build the business because you have agreed to honour the financial costs!

Own - Some solo professionals choose to purchase an office for themselves or one that is large enough so they can rent or lease a portion of it to others. For my first three year lease, I rented the whole office to another professional for scheduled hours. This helped me to pay both the costs of the lease and the utilities so that my monthly expenses were reduced. Doing this also reminded me that I need to take breaks and would schedule them on the days when my renters were using the office.

When you are planning to purchase an office you will need to consider all the "hidden" costs that might not seem evident at first. Parking space, taxes, utilities, renovations and legal costs can surprise you with how quickly they increase your original start-up costs and monthly operating expenses. Owning does allow you the freedom to renovate or change things as well as the power to determine who will use the office and how this will happen. On the other hand, as an owner, you are totally responsible for all of the management and financial commitments.

Some solo professionals use an area in their house to operate their businesses. A home-base office has many advantages. You do not have any expenses for travelling to an office, you can juggle your home and work responsibilities and you will likely be able to write off some of your house expenses on your income tax return. On the other hand, having a business in your house might cause you to be subjected to distractions or the temptation to not work a full day on your business tasks. You might also face some risk to your personal and family safety depending on whether the clients you will be seeing have tendencies towards violence.

Things to consider regarding location

For decades, real estate agents have used the slogan "location, location, location" to remind people of what is important for both residential and business. But it's not just the address that is important. In fact there are a number of things that you need to consider when choosing the location for your business.

Physical location - The first thing that you need to consider is the type of clientele you will serve. The elderly and children often do not have transportation so choosing an office in a newer area may hinder them. I have clients, for example who use the city bus and others who walk to my office for their appointments.

Think about the location you are considering for your office. Are there confusing traffic rings or multi-lane highways that will have to be navigated? Would clients be able to take advantage of good bus schedules or walking paths? What about sidewalks and safe crossings? Is there signage to help the client find your office on their first visit? Would your office be situated in or near residential housing?

No matter how prosperous or popular an area will be in a couple of years, it might not be suitable at this time and your bottom line may suffer if the area is not developed properly. You need to consider convenience for your client when you are choosing an office. It is important to also consider your own needs. If the office is far from your residence, you will experience additional time and travel costs. Living close to the office will not only be convenient but also more cost effective.

Plan how you will be able to help the clients easily find your office. It is a good idea to put a map and clear directions on your website. Make sure you have a bus schedule and an accurate idea of how long it will take to drive from a central, well-known location in the community to your office. Providing this information to the clients will help them to plan and ensure that they arrive right on time for their appointments.

Parking - It is so frustrating to drive around and around and around the block hoping to find a parking place. Your clients will easily become discouraged unless they can find adequate parking. They might also be annoyed if they need to pay for street or lot parking in addition to their appointment fees. Perhaps offering parking passes or giving the client clear directions to free parking will help them to eliminate what might otherwise lead them to book with your competition.

Stairs and handicapped access - Many clients will not be able to book with you unless you have a barrier-free design that accommodates their physical limitations. This includes elevators, wide doorways, low counters and accessible bathroom facilities. I do not do well climbing upstairs and know that if possible, I would definitely book an appointment with someone on the ground floor or go to a building with an elevator rather than face a long flight of stairs. Many Employee Assistance Programs will not sign contracts with you unless your office has handicap access.

Safety and security - Clients will not be eager to go to an office where they think they might be at risk. Before you commit to a location, visit it during the day and at night to see if there are any things that might be dangerous. Construction areas, poor lighting, or gangs might present dangers.

You also need to have a plan in place to protect you and other clients from any risks associated with disgruntled or mentally ill clients.

Having an employee within hearing distance during your sessions or installing a safety buzzer to alert someone else in case of problems are good options.

Safety also involves protecting your reputation. If you are seeing children, for example, it is wise to have a plan in place that would prevent or reduce the chances of your being accused of inappropriate behaviours towards the child.

You will be in your office for many of your waking hours and therefore need to ensure that it offers both convenience and safety for you and your clients.

7 work areas that you might set up

Your business will require that you have several specific facilities each of which has a different purpose. These may be part of a couple of rooms or extend into several rooms. You can begin planning your office by writing down all of the tasks you will perform and then grouping them into work areas.

Administration - You will need to have a place that is quiet where you will answer the telephone, schedule appointments and do bookkeeping. This may be set up in a corner of your client office or a separate room. A desk would be helpful, especially one with drawers to hold supplies. You might decide to use a laptop computer rather than a desktop model so that you can take it with you when you have appointments outside of the office or leave to go home at the end of the day. If you have staff, you will need a separate room for that person and, even if it is very small, it can be set up in an organized and efficient manner.

Reception - You might need an area for clients to wait for their appointment times. This, however, can be arranged creatively. For example, I leave a space of fifteen minutes between appointments so that there isn't much need for anyone to wait. Should someone come early for an appointment, however, they can wait in my multi-purpose room. For years, I didn't have a reception area and just made clients aware of this, asking them to arrive right on time. When I book evening appointments with clients, I make sure they know that they are to wait in their vehicles until their scheduled appointment at which time I unlock the building's outside door for them.

Client office - You will likely spend most of your day in this room and it therefore should be both pleasing and comfortable. Instead of chairs, for example, I have two beautiful loveseats. The lighting is low and there is soft music. Most clients are very impressed and immediately state how relaxing the room feels. Use your personality and practicality to develop a client office that is attractive and useful. For example, I have a telephone with hands-free option so that we can case conference with other professionals during the appointment if necessary. Afghans offer a degree of comfort for those who feel cold when they are sitting and a big basket of stickers brings smiles to the faces of child clients.

Conference and family office - A large round table is a good asset for those who do testing, mediation or family work. I have one that has leaves which can be used to extend its size. Four chairs are usually enough but I also have a couple of extras that can be pulled up to the table for larger groups.

Library - Most professionals have many books, professional magazines and other items that could fit nicely in an organized fashion on portable bookshelves which could be installed in any room. Remember to allow for expansion when you purchase and place them.

Storage - Files need to be locked in order to be confidential. Where you place the cabinets will, of course, depend on your available space. It is extremely important that you have a great deal of expansion as files must be kept for many years, depending on the regulations of your professional body. You will also need storage room for supplies, computer paper and ink, as well as other documents that are important to your business. Because I am also an author, I rented a separate office in the same building where I can store books, shipping materials and other important equipment. Your storage does not necessarily have to be in the same area but make sure that it is convenient or you will soon be resenting all the carrying you will need to do.

Bathroom and lunch room facilities - You might need to share a bathroom with others in your building or perhaps use your client or administration space for your lunch or coffee breaks rather than pay higher rent for a large space. A small bar fridge and microwave oven are wonderful assets that will allow you to save money by staying in the office rather than going out to restaurants for food and beverages.

Be creative when you set up your office space. For example, I have a very small administrative office as well as one client office. My multi-purpose room houses the library, filing cabinets, fridge, microwave, storage cabinets and round table set. We can use this office for storage, breaks, groups or study. Sometimes I even use it as a reception area for clients who arrive extremely early for their appointments.

Remember your office needs to be convenient and well-organized. If you put the time and effort into planning and setting up in order to accomplish these goals, you will not only save time but also feel proud of the space that you have created.

Putting your personality into your surroundings

It is interesting that people tend to design their homes as a reflection of their personalities, tastes and interests but then set up an office that is very impersonal. Because you spend most of your waking hours at the office, it is also important that it is a comfortable and convenient place that reflects who you are. Consider your likes and dislikes, the work you will be doing, and your preferred style when setting up the place that you will work.

Following are 30 things that I have in my office that help to make it a "home away from home":

1. Colour - My favourite colour is purple. I have therefore chosen a light pinky-mauve colour for all the walls and have accessorized with white and purple. I use dimmed lighting for the therapy room. The impact on others is amazing as the colours provide a calming effect and an atmosphere they didn't expect.

2. Style - People laugh when I state that I set up the office in the style of "classy hotel lobby". Rather than choosing typical office furniture, I have white loveseats, lots of wood, cupboards with doors and accessories you would likely expect more in a home than in an office. Afghans, end tables, lamps and floral arrangements help the clients to relax very quickly. Wall hangings and pictures each have personal meaning and include not only my degrees and licenses but also personal photographs and artwork.

3. Music - My client office has a stereo which holds five CDs that play songs randomly. I only play soft, calm tunes that are relaxing. Classical music doesn't work because the volume changes are too drastic. Also, I never play songs I know because then I tend to hum or sing along.

4. Conveniences - A small bar fridge, microwave and a few china cups help to make the office feel more like home for me and allow me to serve a beverage to the clients.

5. Library - I LOVE books and have hired grandchildren and contract staff to categorize and computerize everything so things are easy to find. I don't ever lend books or other items to anyone, however, as no matter how trustworthy your clientele or other professionals, some things are never returned.

6. Computers - I enjoy using computers for Internet marketing, research and administrative tasks. Because of this, I have a desktop for me to use at the office and a laptop at home which also allows remote access to the office computer. I have saved many trips to the office and much time by having this networking system.

7. Self-care items - An alarm clock in the therapy room allows me to take a short nap when there is an opportunity to do so in the middle of the day. I also keep a few items such as a can of almonds, individual yogurt cups, a supply of bottled water and my favourite soft drink in the fridge for break time. A small bag of personal care items such as makeup, deodorant, toothpaste and brush and generic medications are available for freshening up and special circumstances. It is also important to have room fresheners handy

as sometimes you might have a client arrive straight from the barn or with a baby who decided to dirty their diaper during the appointment time.

8. Special client items - I tend to use baskets to store stickers which I give out to children and referral brochures and business cards for adults. Besides this, I have a number of safe toys and children's books to occupy children who accompany clients when the babysitter cancels at the last minute.

When it comes to decorating your office, there is really no right or wrong way to do it. I have had clients make both positive and negative comments over the years and the odd time I have made an adjustment considering what was said. Your business adventure, however, is made more interesting when you incorporate your personality into the environment.

When planning your office, keep in mind that it should be a wonderful place that you and your clients can share in comfort.

How to make excellent first impressions

First impressions are lasting and the first contact that your client has with your office will not only remain in their memories but also influence their future involvement with you. There are several no or low-cost things that you can do to ensure that your client has a good first impression of you and your business.

Marketing materials - Your office is extended into the world through the marketing materials you prepare. When prospects search for you on the Internet will they find a professional and informative website? Is your telephone book advertising appealing? Are your brochures and business cards nicely designed and printed on quality paper? Are your other marketing materials ones of which you can be proud?

Everything that has your name on it is part of the "brand" that you are creating and, as such, is a preview to the relationship which you will be developing with the client and other professionals.

Reputation - The things that people say about you will either help to build your business or restrict it. People who know, like and trust you will refer others to you through word of mouth. Guard and treasure a good reputation with utmost diligence.

Telephone contact - When people call your office they may get a voice mail message before actually talking with you or your staff. Use a friendly but professional tone on you voice mail recording. Remember to state the name of the business, open office hours, encouragement for callers to leave a message, information about when the call will be returned and give thanks in advance for the caller's message. If you have a website, you can offer them the address so they can read about you and the business while waiting for a response.

I do not have a receptionist in the office with me so my voice mail message clearly states that the telephone will not be answered. This is followed by a promise that the person's call will be returned by the end of the next business day. Many people have told me how much they appreciate this information as they then do not have to keep trying to reach me or wonder when someone will answer their call.

Conversations involving callers and you or your staff - Offering both respect and information in a polite fashion from the very first contact will help your potential clients to have a preview of the services you will provide for them in the future. Listen carefully to ensure that you understand what the person needs and wants. If a referral would be appropriate, offer it. Be helpful but do not do any of the work that you would normally do in an appointment time. You want to encourage the person come into the office so you can offer good service that is billable.

Your Reception Area - When someone walks into your office will they feel comfortable? I still talk about the beauty of an accountant's office that I visited a few years ago. The colours and simplicity were stunning. In fact, one paint colour is usually the same price as another paint colour but the differences in their effect can be astounding.

A reception area that is free of clutter and protective of confidential information is appealing to those who enter your office. Ensure that there is appropriate seating and that the room is soundproof. Even the smell of stale smoke can turn a client off. Every sense is at play in analyzing the environment - sight, sound, touch, smell and even taste can be in play when it comes to first impressions. For example, even offering a bottle of water for the client who is waiting can be a very kind gesture that will be locked in memory for them. Many clients are nervous or unsure about being in your office in the first place. Everything that you can do to relax them is positive.

Appearance - As a solo professional, you are the business. What your client sees and hears is key to how they feel about the experience. Your staff also represents you. It is therefore important that you and the staff dress in a professional manner. Consider taking a course or hiring an expert to help you with your wardrobe, hair and other grooming. You might suggest a uniform for your staff members or have a conversation with them that outlines your expectations regarding appearance. It doesn't usually cost a great deal to be clean and tidy and you don't need a huge expensive wardrobe to dress appropriately. It is far easier, however, to talk about this when you hire staff than have to carry on a conversation at a later point.

Attitude - How you view the world and treat others will go a long way in building your business and relationships with friends, family, clients or other professionals. I think that having a good attitude is like carrying a full glass of water that splashes on others as you travel through life. Problems which are viewed as opportunities or challenges are more easily handled and simple words of hope can help improve another person's life.

One of my goals is that no matter who I am with during the day or where we are, the other person will walk away and say "that was the best part of my day".

As a solo professional, you are the one who is responsible for the environment in your office. This can be a daunting task but, with thought, planning and good communication, can make every day easier and more peaceful for those who cross your path.

Using your telephone to build a good image

I know many professionals who state that they are annoyed by the number of telephone calls they receive, frustrated with voice mail and disgusted when they can't get through to people they want to speak with. There are some techniques, however, that will help you to build good relationships and get the information you need in a timely fashion.

Your voice mail message - When someone calls your office they will be pleased to hear a professional business message. Invite them to leave a message for you, explain when you will return their call and direct them to your website. They will likely be able to answer some of their own questions by reviewing the information you have included on the website. If they know when to expect your return call and also hear the voice of a friendly and polite individual they will look forward to hearing from you. All of this builds rapport and is much more effective than exchanging several messages where you each state your name, number and the words"Call me back".

Leaving messages for professionals- "Telephone tag" is a frustrating and time-consuming activity. When you need information from someone, leave a clear and detailed message for them that states exactly what you need to know, when you need the information and how it can be sent to you. Be sure that you slowly and clearly give your name, telephone number and website address so that they can respond appropriately.

You usually do not need to speak directly to people in order to get information. Just leave them a message that clearly outlines what you need. This works extremely well when you want to check with accounting departments about unpaid invoices or when you need specific reports that can be sent to you by email attachment. You can leave a message listing all the invoice numbers, dates and amounts and then ask them to leave you a message indicating when and how they will be paid. Or you can request a specific report and ask the other person to send it directly to you through your email address. Keep it simple and you will not only save time but receive respect from the person who you called as their time is also valuable.

Leaving messages for clients - Many clients who call you will want to know basic information that you have included on your website. When you return their call, you can leave them a message to direct them to that website. Also indicate when you will be available for any questions that are still unanswered after they have reviewed your site.

There are times that established clients call stating "I just want to book an appointment". If I have an idea of their preferences, I will leave a message offering them two or three available times and ask them to confirm by voice mail. This saves several calls back and forth to accomplish the same results.

Many of my clients prefer to use email for booking or changing appointments. This is another great time saver.

Return all calls in a timely manner - My voice mail states "We will return your call by the end of the next business day" and I ensure that this is done. I have even called clients from as far away as Jamaica in order to honour that statement. Now I have a virtual assistant who regularly listens to and return calls, even when I am out of country.

Checking your voice mail remotely and returning calls by cellphones allow even more communication opportunities!

Also, remember that it is better to leave a positive message on a machine than to keep trying without leaving a message. The person who initially left you their message will respect the fact that you tried to reach them.

The telephone is a "tool" and like any tool it can be used improperly or with expertise. It is usually just a few little techniques that move you from one category to the other.

10 reasons people will want to work for you

We live in a world where many people are unhappy. Some do not like their jobs or do not trust others. Many have been hurt in personal relationship problems and allow this to carry over into the workplace. Because of these things, prospective employees are usually looking for an opportunity to work with someone who will provide a healthy environment and also recognize their contributions.

We might think that this is common sense but sometimes the things that seem to be common sense aren't all that common.

Following are ten things that people are usually searching for in their work relationships.

1. **Honesty** - All we have to do is listen to the latest news reports to know that there is a great deal of dishonesty in the world - even from people and organizations that we thought we could trust. When you tell the truth and live in an honest manner, people feel safe and secure.

2. **Respect** - Self-respect, respect for others and respect for our world are all important. Those who treat those people and things that are around them in a respectable manner are very attractive people.

3. **Example** – It is a sad thing that there are very few people who can name a person who they view as their "hero". We all need leaders and people who can be our role-models in how to live well.

4. **Integrity** - A person who has wholesome and ethical virtues is said to be of good character. Most people want to deal with someone who has trustworthy morals.

5. **Appreciation** - Two of the rarest words in the English language are "thank you". All of us want to be appreciated for who we are and the work we do.

6. **Clear Communication** - Relationships and businesses are built to last when people are able to communicate clearly and honestly. Those who can relay a message or facilitate a dialogue are valued in society.

7. **Fairness** - Each person has his or her own definition of fairness. John F. Kennedy stated "Life isn't fair". It is very rare for someone to be considered to be fair by their peers and what one person defines as "fair" is not necessarily what another person thinks is "fair". You will have to work at it on an ongoing basis.

8. **Attitude** - Your approach to life and the positive attitude that you demonstrate to the world is a rare treasure that others will want to be around.

9. **Productivity** - If you are moving forward in your life and developing a prosperous business, others will take interest. Everyone loves a winner!

10. **Hope** - President Obama built his entire campaign on a foundation that promised hope. We all want to think that things can be better than they are and be associated with someone who knows how to make that happen.

People usually want to work and be around others who have embraced strong morals and developed healthy lifestyles. They want genuineness.

If you were applying for a job right now would you want to work with someone who has the same characteristics and behaviours that you demonstrate? Are you attractive to the type of employees that you want to work in your business?

If not, maybe it's time to make some changes.

What are your staffing options?

"I'm forming a committee to create a task force to choose
a team leader to assemble a board to hire the best people
to determine the fastest way to deal with the problem."

Operating as a solo professional can drain time and energy. You may
feel you do not have the skills or ability to operate the business on your
own or you may decide that it is better for you to earn more money
by focusing on your clients and hiring others to do the rest. There are
several options for you to consider regarding how the administrative
part of your business will be run.

Not having staff means that everything falls in your lap. You will need
a myriad of skills and energy in order to see the clients and also do all
the ordering, bookkeeping, scheduling, and what seems like millions
of others tasks that keep the business running efficiently. It is especially
important for you to have a backup if you are ill or away from the office
for travel or other reasons. At one point, I found myself calling clients
from Jamaica because I didn't have staff to return telephone calls!

When you don't have any staff, you risk the chance of losing income because of the time taken from your client work or the errors that you might make. You also probably don't have all the latest information for government payments and income tax submission or the computer savvy to streamline operations. The biggest risk for your business is that you will burn out or be ill for some time and not be able to continue with the practice. Remember, you are the business so you need to protect yourself.

Project Contracts are a good way to get tasks done when specific expertise is required. Asking another professional to give you a quote for the work will help you to decide if you want to invest in this manner and allows you to plan and incorporate the costs into your budget.

You can negotiate an hourly rate or project rate. For example, I hire an accountant by the hour to do all my government work (sales tax, payroll submission and annual income tax). She charges me by the hour for the first two and on a set fee schedule for the annual return. When I wanted to have my library books sorted, categorized, computerized and shelved, I hired someone by the hour to do this.

Contracting services can be a very cost-effective way to hire people with expertise to complete projects for you. You might want someone to set up a website, update your filing system, create marketing materials or develop a business plan for you.

Think of the things that you promise yourself that you will do "some day" and consider contracting them out to people who will get them done for you. Your mind will be relieved and you will be able to use the time that you might have spent tackling them to see more clients. Before you know it, you will have earned enough extra to pay for the contract.

Regular Contract Hours - I have tried all types of arrangements for office staff and find that hiring for a flexible number of contracted hours at an hourly rate works best for me. This way, I can adjust the hours that I need my assistant according to my needs.

Because there are no employee benefits I have slightly increased the rate that I would otherwise pay. Also, I save time that I would invest in doing paperwork because this is a contract rather than an employee payroll situation.

At the present time, I have a virtual assistant who has remote access to the business voice mail and the computer. She calls into the office a couple of times a day and then returns all the telephone messages. She documents each call on her laptop and then prints a copy of her contact on the office printer for the paper file.

Part-time Staff - If you are hiring someone as a part-time employee you will need to define what part-time means and what, if any benefits are included in your agreement with that person. It is best to put this in writing and have it available to share with the prospective employee at hiring.

In the past, I have prepared a written agreement which the employee and I sign and date.

Full-time Staff - This is probably the most costly way of hiring and can be the most wasteful - especially if the employee doesn't have enough to do during the day. S/he would likely expect employee benefits and paid holidays as well as sick leave. If they do not have all the skills you need, then you might still need to hire a project contract person for specific projects.

Before you hire anyone, you need to know exactly what needs to be done in your office. Write out a list of all the tasks. Then determine what tasks you will do yourself. At this point, consider hiring someone who is best suited to complete the rest of the tasks that are on the list.

Make sure that you check references offered by prospective employees. Their perceptions might not be at all like the perceptions which former employers have regarding their knowledge, skills and work ethic. Before you call the references, write out a list of questions that you want to ask.

Hiring staff is a big commitment. When you are away from the office you will be paying that person and when they are away from the office you will be paying that person. If they make an error, it will be a reflection on your business.

You will need to be sure that you can clearly outline what tasks need to be done and then carefully choose a person who will be able to do them in an efficient and accurate manner. You will also need to be compatible with that person so that your working relationship is a positive one.

How to develop job descriptions for staff

Before you hire anyone in your private practice, it is important that you determine what that employee or contract person will be doing for you. There are several steps in the process that will help you to ensure that you have hired the right person to do the work.

1. Sit down in a quiet place where you can think, plan and work without interruption

2. On a piece of paper write down all of the things that only you can do. These will be the services which only you hold a license to perform, the management tasks that you need to monitor (such as bank accounts and business statements) as well as the personal choice decisions that need to be made (choosing decor, hiring contractors or developing marketing plans).

3. On a different piece of paper list all the other things that need to be done - but not necessarily by you. They might include things such as ordering supplies, answering the telephone, scheduling appointments, filing, organizing information, making bank deposits, delivering mail or maintaining equipment. It is important that you list everything no matter how small the task may seem.

4. Draw a vertical line down the middle of a third sheet of paper. On the left hand side start sorting the tasks into logical groupings

(tasks out of the office, computer tasks, filing and organization tasks etc)

5. On the right-hand side of the third paper list the skills or abilities that a person would need in order to accomplish the task. For example, someone who will be preparing and making bank deposits will need computer skills, math skills and either a vehicle or the ability to walk to the bank to physically make the deposit.

6. When you have completed this use a coloured pen to mark the amount of time that you think each category would take to accomplish. Some tasks might need to be done on a daily basis while others might be weekly or monthly activities.

7. Consider which if any of the tasks could be contracted by another professional such as an accountant or lawyer.

8. Once you have calculated the approximate number of hours required to complete all of the tasks, calculate the costs to hire someone to do this. You will likely want to pay more than the minimum wage in order to get a skilled person.

    Contact an Employment Agency to ask about the rate per hour that would be reasonable. In fact, the agency may even have someone who would be suitable for the position.

9. If there are tasks that could be completed by a Virtual Assistant you might want to consider this and begin to research the best match.

When you have finally identified all the tasks that you would like someone to do for hire, you can type or write them out in simple but detailed fashion. I usually attach this Job Description to the other documents that I prepare when hiring staff and ensure that we each have copies so our expectations match.

Writing a Job Description is a rather simple task after you have determined what you need to have done that you will not be doing yourself.

Hiring someone with skill in the task areas will allow you peace of mind as well as the opportunity to work additional hours seeing clients. In fact, the amount you can earn in one hour with clients will likely pay for several hours of staffing. Just make sure that your staff is clear about what needs to be done and the timeframe for completing the tasks.

What documents are needed when you hire staff?

When you hire employees or set up staff contracts, there are a few important documents that you will need to prepare. Ensure that you and the other person each receive a copy of the following:

Letter of Offer - You do not usually need a lawyer to draw up a formal document but instead can prepare this yourself as long as you make sure that you include everything that is necessary. The letter should be dated and addressed to the person who is being contracted or hired.

Include the following in the letter:

1. Their full name and address
2. Their date of birth
3. The starting date for services
4. The number of hours and rate per hour or total amount to be paid for a project
5. The expected end date of the contract (if there is one) or project completion date
6. Details of the things that the employee or contracted person will or will not receive (benefits, sick leave or holidays)
7. Hours of work (if they are to be regular)
8. A statement indicating that there will be two attachments (Job Description and Confidentiality Agreement)
9. Two blank lines for the person to sign and date the letter before returning the letter to you
10. Two blank lines for you to sign and date.

Make a photocopy of the letter for the other person and one for their personnel file which you are creating.

Job Description - Attach a very detailed and clearly written description of the tasks and duties that you have reviewed with the person before hiring them.

Confidentiality Agreement - Prepare a document which clearly outlines the importance of confidentiality and the consequences for breaching. You will need to have this signed by your new employee after you have had a discussion in which you explain exactly what is expected and how to protect the information of both you and your clients.

Banking Letter - If the person you are hiring will be responsible for making bank deposits, your bank will need a letter to indicate this. Be very clear in the letter that the named person has your authority to ask for information and make deposits but NOT to make decisions on your behalf. The original of the letter will go to the bank and a copy will be kept in the employee's personnel file or the contract file.

Change letters - If you decide to change the rate of pay, hours of work or job description, a full updated letter will need to be prepared and signed by both of you and a copy kept by each.

Any mandatory government forms - Ensure that any important government forms are completed and filed.

I keep a separate personnel file for each of the people who I hire with an appropriate label and all the documents listed above for each person. Documentation prevents the "I didn't know" excuse from occurring.

3 mistakes employers make

When you hire staff or sign a contract to work with another professional there are times that things don't go well and, in fact, the relationship might end up in frustration and division. There are three mistakes that employers frequently make which contribute to the problems.

Breaking promises - When you hire someone and offer them salary or contract fees you have made a commitment to them. They are counting on you and trust that you will honour your words. Frequently, I hear of employers who do not follow the agreements or promises they made. They do not pay the amount they owe another person or do not pay it within the timeframe laid out. Sometimes they try to change the terms by lowering commission rates, adding conditions or cancelling benefits. Even something that can seem insignificant to the employer might be a huge breach of trust for the other person. Many of these situations result in legal actions. All of them result in distrust, disrespect, and loss of reputation.

If you want to retain dignity and maintain your integrity, do what you have promised.

Making assumptions - When you think that the other person has the knowledge, skills or abilities to do a job and do not explain your expectations, you are setting up both them and you for failure. Thinking that you know what the other person is thinking is probably going to result in problems. Assuming that you know how things will turn out can be a form of arrogance. I once heard another person break the word assume into pieces by saying "it makes an ass out of u and me". How true!

If you want to have an honest relationship with people and situations, do not make assumptions.

Not communicating - Relationships are build and enhanced through communication. You can share ideas through dialogue or written forms of communication. It is important that there are two sides to a conversation, however, or it is merely a monologue. Your employee has a perspective, information, and ways that are hidden to you unless you take the time and interest to find out what they are. Your employees and contracted workers are on your side and have much to offer you but they need to know that you value them and want to have a good working relationship with them. They need to know that you are open to hearing what they have to say without rejection or criticism. They cannot read your mind and it is therefore up to you to have conversations with them so that you can both strive towards the same goals.

If you want to have good working relationships with others, you need to develop two-way communications with them.

Keeping your promises, avoiding assumptions and communicating will help you, your staff and your business to grow separately and together in a healthy and trusting manner.

Stopping and preventing workplace bullying

As a solo professional you are responsible for what happens in your practice. This includes the way that people treat each other. Stopping and preventing workplace bullying is an important aspect of protecting your business and you therefore need to understand it and the strategies that will be effective to prevent it.

Workplace bullying provides a strong threat for individual employees as well as organizations as it can jeopardize the psychological and financial well-being of those involved.

Rick Brenner, of *Chaco Canyon Consulting* in Boston, Massachusetts, whose work focuses on improving personal and organizational effectiveness, claims:

Workplace bullies are probably the organization's most expensive employees. They reduce the effectiveness not only of their targets, but also of bystanders and of the organization as a whole (2004).

The problem is not isolated to one country or continent. The *Australian Council of Trade Unions* (ACTU), for example, used workplace surveys to research workplace bullying and the results were shocking: Over half the respondents (53%) to the union survey report an unhappy oppressive workplace, and 54% say that the intimidating behaviour; shouting, ordering and belittling people happens in their workplaces. Almost a third report abusive language. The ACTU estimates that: 350,000 people are subjected to long term bullying in Australia, while 2.5 million experience some aspect of bullying over the course of their working lives. Workplace bullying may be costing Australian businesses up to $3 billion annually.

And the problem can be found in every country of the world!

There are many definitions of the term workplace bullying but everyone agrees that there are three different groups who contribute to this. Each can create or help to stop the problem. They are the bully, the target and the organization that allows it to occur.

As a solo professional you will need to understand issues and strategies to deal with workplace bullying and prevent a toxic environment from occurring. This will allow you to create a healthy workplace which has zero tolerance for abuse. Information and training are available for those who do not have much knowledge about workplace bullying. It is up to you to do the research in order to find ways to ensure that you and your employees are safe.

Planning Your Success

- ❑ Will you rent, lease or own?

- ❑ What location have you chosen for your business?

- ❑ Which of the seven recommended areas will you set up?

- ❑ How will your personality be reflected in your environment?

- ❑ What will you do to make excellent first impressions?

- ❑ How will you use your telephone to build a good image?

- ❑ Are there 10 reasons why people will want to work for you?

- ❑ Have you chosen your best staffing option?

- ❑ Do you have written Job Descriptions for you and your staff?

- ❑ Are documents prepared so that you can begin hiring staff?

- ❑ Do you know the 3 mistakes employers make?

- ❑ Do you have a strategy to avoid these mistakes?

- ❑ Do you have a policy to deal with workplace bullying?

Notes:

Chapter Four

CUSTOMIZING SYSTEMS TO FUNCTION EFFECTIVELY

Three necessary systems for your business

Think about your body. It consists of a number of parts that all work together in a very intricate and efficient manner. Each part is absolutely necessary for health and life. You do not have more parts than you need but instead have exactly the right number – each with a specific function. If there is a problem with one part, the whole body suffers.

Business systems act in a similar manner. They help you to do specific tasks in an organized manner in order to have a healthy business. You need to have specific systems, each with its own role, that will work together.

The *Merriam-Webster Online Dictionary* defines a "system" as "a regularly interacting or interdependent group of items forming a unified whole" and "an organized or established procedure".

If you invest time and energy in setting up at least three systems in your business, you will be richly rewarded as things will then operate with efficiency and accuracy. You will save both time and effort each day.

Technological system - It is amazing at how quickly technology changes. Just when I felt that I had mastered email, I learned that my grandchildren do not use it and actually view email as "outdated". They communicate with texting and through Facebook.

We live in an age where there is new technology being introduced to the market every single week and it would be very difficult, if not impossible, to keep up with all the latest options that are available.

On the other hand, very few businesses operate without some technology and it is important that you do take advantage of at least a few options that the world of technology has for you.

Recently my eleven year old grandson who is an iphone expert came to spend a week with me. He couldn't understand why I knew so little about technology. I pointed to a cupboard above the refrigerator and asked him to tell me what was stored in it. He looked puzzled and answered "I don't know". I explained that this is how I feel about new technology. Sometimes I just don't know what is available let alone how it might help me.

I often explain my limited knowledge of computers as "unconscious incompetence". This means that I don't know what I don't know. It's kind of like being dropped into Italy without knowing any Italian or the customs of the country. Everything would be awkward at first.

You do not necessarily need the newest computer on the market or the most complex software in order to operate your business. What you do need is technology that works to help you save time and effort. And you cannot make good choices unless you research what is available.

There are a number of things to consider when you are choosing the parts for your technological system including the costs, features and benefits you desire.

Technology should only be purchased if it fills a legitimate business need. Speak with an expert or consultant about the problems that you are experiencing and the tasks that you regularly do. That person will help to match your needs with the appropriate solutions.

You need to be careful about purchasing exactly what you need rather than what a sales person thinks you need or tells you that you need. Just because something has games or "bells and whistles" that impress the sales clerk doesn't mean that you need these. In fact, buying equipment that you want instead of what you need might even distract you from doing your business. Many people are mesmerized by social media or gaming and allow them to steal time from tasks that should be done instead.

Buying a computer system is like buying a car. You don't usually buy a Lamborghini when you are looking for a family car. You consider the needs of the family, the price you can afford and the way that the vehicle will be used before making your selection. Purchase your computer with the same consideration and you will be likely be pleased with the results.

Make sure that you learn about different types of software and how to use them to streamline your daily activities. Remember, computers are a business tool and are only effective if you know how to use them properly. Investing a few hours in training at the beginning can save you hundreds of hours throughout the year.

Bookkeeping system - Businesses that do not have a system for keeping track of finances usually do not survive very long.

You need to keep accurate information about the business income, expenses, assets and liabilities in order to make appropriate financial decisions. Governments require that you submit accurate documentation and remittances for payroll and annual income tax returns. If you have a computerized system which you update each day, your year-end work will be done for you without any effort.

Some people use manual bookkeeping systems but most businesses prefer to set up computerized systems. I have found that having a computerized system that I can operate myself and pay for on a monthly business is extremely efficient and very cost effective.

A few years ago I hired a bookkeeper who would come to the office every quarter and enter all my manual figures into a computer system. We had it backwards! I realized that it would have made much more sense to do computer entries as they occurred and then print out reports.

Next I hired a full-time assistant who really didn't understand bookkeeping software or accounting principles. She spent considerable hours doing things by hand and then trying to coordinate her system with the software. I trusted her to take care of things for me but there never seemed to be much money in the account. Once I started asking good questions and reviewing the figures it didn't take long for me to realize that accounts receivables had skyrocketed and expenses were at an unacceptable high. The harder I worked, the more problems there seemed to be as my staff didn't know what she was doing!

At that point I decided that I needed to take full responsibility for the financial aspects of my business and monitor things very closely until things were under control again.

I didn't know much about financial software but watched the training videos that were part of the package. When I got to the point that I clearly understood all aspects of my financial situation and the software at a basic level, I had my son streamline everything and teach me how to use the system properly with the least amount of effort. He set up short-cuts and helped me to prepare "cheat sheets" for procedures that I needed to do once in a while rather than daily. I taped these to the front of the printer where they could be found without any searching.

I am proud of the fact that I can now prepare a *Customer Sales Receipt* with just a few clicks of the mouse or view any number of reports within seconds. In fact, I now do all the financial work other than the government reporting which I leave to an accountant who I pay by the hour.

There are several things that you, as the business owner must do before you can enjoy an efficient bookkeeping system. First you need to understand your business and be well-versed enough to discuss all lines of each computerized report with your accountant. Secondly, you need to ensure that the software which you purchase is set up properly so that it records everything in the right accounts and saves you time. Finally, you need to learn how to use all features of the software. This way, if you change staff or need to know a specific piece of information, you are able to do what needs to be done. You may even choose to follow my example and do the entries yourself rather than hiring staff.

Remember, this is your business and it is therefore very important that you understand all of the financial aspects of it. Like a former United States President once said "The buck stops here".

Filing system - Even though there are many efforts to "go green" and protect the environment by using as little paper as possible, most businesses have paper files for at least some aspects of their work.

I have client files, financial files and topical files besides my computer systems and have found that sometimes it is just easier to look at information on paper than on a computer screen. For example: the clients often ask questions about their last appointment or whether expected documentation has been received. By having a paper file with me in the therapy room, I am able to quickly find the information that they request or add paper documents that they give me to the file without having to scan them.

I have chosen to colour-code my files and this makes it so much easier to identify the specific system that they belong in. For example, financial files are green, client files burgundy, speaking engagements are blue and topical files are tan. This practice saves me considerable time when I am either looking for files or replacing them in cabinets.

There are so many other systems that can be created to improve your business practices. Besides the above, you might set up systems for marketing, client process, personnel, or a multitude of other topics. Besides this, you might want to take some time each month to review the systems that you have been using and see how you can improve them. Just remember that the goals are to be professional and save time.

Systems allow you to do the same procedures over and over again with positive results and although they often take time and effort to develop, you will quickly recognize the benefits they bring to your office.

Technology should make your life easier

Many people are fascinated with technology and actually fool themselves into believing that they need certain things for their business. They think that having a business justifies investing a great deal of money into computer "toys". This practice can not only drain the company of capital but also steal hours of your time that might otherwise be used to increase income and profits.

When used as a tool rather than a toy, however, technology can make your life much easier. Consider how the following items might help you in your business:

Telephone - There are a number of options available when it comes to what type of telephone system you will use.

One of my psychologist friends uses only a cellphone with voice mail to operate a very profitable private practice. This gives him the opportunity to check messages and return calls no matter where he is at the time.

I also have a cellphone but use it only for personal calls. A landline telephone with hands-free option in my client office makes it possible to have telephone conferences with other professionals while our client is in the room.

My Virtual Assistant has remote access to my business' voice mail system and a cordless phone to schedule all my appointments from her house which is more than two hours from my office.

Cellphones and iphones that have built in cameras for photos or videos, email/Internet availability and a myriad of applications can be tempting but they may increase your purchase price and monthly expenses while not actually being business necessities.

The important thing when it comes to choosing your telephone system is that you know your business needs.

Begin making good choices by doing some homework. Write down all the features that you need for the business (not just the wants). Then do some research – either on the Internet or in person at a store. Learn about the options and costs for available choices that will meet your needs.

Once you decide on the type of system you will purchase, make sure that you do cost comparisons through both manufacturers and retailers. Sometimes companies offer specials that include free services or free equipment for customers. Even stores that carry the same products might sell them at different prices. If you are not in a hurry, you will likely also notice that just before a company launches a new product, the prices of items that are on the store shelf drop drastically. August back-to-school sales might also provide you with a good price for both equipment and software.

Be very careful when signing up for long distance or cellphone plans though as there can be a great deal of difference in the costs and terms that are available. You do need to read the fine print and understand the commitment you are making before you sign any contract. Research is not only a good idea – it is necessary – if you want to get the best deal possible and not get locked into a commitment that you cannot fulfill.

Computer - It may seem that desktop computers are "a thing of the past" but I actually like the one that I have in my administration office. It has a large screen which makes everything easy to view. Because I don't want or need to carry it anywhere having a stationary setup works well for me.

I also have a laptop though that I use at home for projects. Remote control access to my office computer allows me to view everything on the laptop. This is a wonderful setup which saves me what would otherwise be many trips to the office.

My Virtual Assistant also uses a laptop and remote access to the office computer for scheduling appointments. She then sends notes about her activities to my email for viewing and to the office printer so a copy can be placed on the paper file.

When it comes to software, we chose packages that offer email, spreadsheet, word processing and bookkeeping functions. Rather than buying an intact packaged bookkeeping program, I purchased a monthly plan so that the software developer can regularly send me updates. This means that I always have the most up-to-date applications and information.

I have two office printers and many times have been so thankful that this is the case – especially when one is not functioning or out of ink. One is a good coloured Laser printer and the other is a FAX machine that accommodates scanning for thick books. I also have an "older" printer at home just to save me trips to the office when I am working at home.

Technology that is set up properly with your business needs in mind will save you several hours each week. All it takes is a willingness to do some research, skills to do customization and a little bit of training!

Bookkeeping systems that are vital to your business

If you do not have a good bookkeeping system it is very easy to lose track of your finances and not even know how your business is doing. You will also waste a great deal of time trying to figure things out when it comes to month end or income tax time.

You can use a manual system but will likely find that a good computerized system will soon pay for itself just in the time that you will save.

A computerized system allows you to set up customer files which will store names, addresses, contact information and notes about each of the people or organizations in your customer base. You can also set up Vendors and customize accounts that will be needed for your financial reports.

Following are the basic functions or sub-systems that are important for your business:

Income - You will need to record all of the money that comes into your business. Accurate records include details about sales, interest earned, refunds received as well as any other sources of income.

Some clients will pay you on the same day that you provided them with goods and services. You will receive their money and offer them a sales receipt.

Accounts Receivable - Contracted services are usually invoiced for what they owe you. You not only need to know who owes you money but also how long it has been that the amount has been due. Sending out statements with interest charges by email or snail mail reminds those who owe money of the balance due and the delinquency period.

Banking - Your bank will likely provide you with a deposit book and bag which you can use to make deposits. If your financial operations are computerized, there will be a function that allows you to receive money on account, deposit it to the appropriate account and print out the deposit slip.

Expenses - When you order or purchase items from vendors you will need to record the amount that you owe and then pay it by cash, cheque, electronic payment or credit card. It is important to sort the expenses into categories (accounts) so that you know how much you have spent in each at the end of the year.

Computerized bookkeeping packages allow you to enter information about vendors and also remind you of the date that payment is due for bills you have entered.

Reports - Most computer software programs allow you to view or print standardized reports or to customize reports in order to obtain the specific information. For example, you can view or print Accounts Receivables, Income and Expense reports, Balance sheets or a number of other helpful reports.

Asset and Liability Records - The things that your business owns and the debts it owes are important figures not only for income tax purposes but also when it comes to determining the financial health of your business. You will likely want to set up a schedule with your accountant that will allow for depreciation of business assets over time.

Payroll - If you or any of your staff is on salary, you will need to accurately record gross income, required deductions and net payouts. Remittances will also need to be made to the government or other organizations on behalf of employees.

Financial Statements - Your accountant will prepare your annual Financial Statements from the information that you have recorded throughout the year and provide you with copies of your Income and Expense Statement, Balance Sheet, Net worth Statement and income tax forms.

But you shouldn't have to wait until your accountant shows up to know how you and your business are doing. Because I do all the financial entries in my business on a daily basis I always know the bank balance, receipts and expenses for the day and how this compares with the previous month and year.

Having good business financial information allows you to feel confident and in control of your situation.

As a solo professional it is therefore very important that you at least review reports on a regular basis and know what your financial situation is at all times. This practice will allow you to make good decisions as well as the necessary adjustments to improve your bottom line on an ongoing basis.

Filing systems

There are several different types of filing systems that can be used in your business to keep things organized and easy to find. Of course, the more paper you use, the more filing cabinets you will need.

I recommend that you choose a different colour for each filing system. This provides you with a visual reminder of where the file belongs.

Following are some of the systems which I have found are helpful in my private practice:

Client Filing System - I have tried a number of different ways of keeping these but have found that the best is to use letter sized folders with self-sticking fasteners on each side. The file label has three rows. The top row has the client's surname (in capital letters) followed by a comma and the first name(s). The second row has a coding system we use that is formed by using the year and month that the client file was opened as well as the number that indicates how many referrals have been received in the year to date. For example, a client referral received on October 11th might appear as 10-11-156.

I have a two-drawer vertical cabinet with legal-sized hanging file folders for active clients which I store in alphabetical order. Because you will receive a number of files over time you therefore need a system that will accommodate and hold them according to professional standards. I have a storage area with locked cabinets where I keep "inactive" files for the ten years required by my regulatory body.

Financial Files - As my business has grown significantly I have had to divide the various aspects of the financial accounting into smaller systems. Initially, I had files for Income, Expenses, Assets, Liabilities, Banking, income tax and Reports but have expanded this into sub-sections for ease in filing and retrieving information.

Different coloured folders for each and separate filing drawers to hold them help to keep things in order.

At the end of each year, I transfer information that needs to be kept from these files into banker's boxes which are housed in a storage area. Marking the year clearly on the outside of the box allows me to find what I need with little effort.

Topical Files - Over the years I have collected a great number of wonderful articles and handouts. These have been sorted into subject groups which are filed alphabetically. An index in the front of each drawer facilitates finding items more quickly. One of my goals is to go through these files, shred the articles that I no longer want and scan the articles that I want to keep in order to save physical space.

Correspondence and General Information - There always seem to be things that you want to keep that don't seem to fit into the above systems. I have a binder where I alphabetically file inquiries or requests that come in from individuals who do not become active clients as well as a drawer for miscellaneous correspondence.

Do not get too sophisticated when it comes to a filing system. The idea is to ensure that the things you keep really need to be kept and then can be found easily when needed. The more complex you make it, the more difficult it can be to maintain.

Filing systems can either waste time or save time depending on how they are set up. It is therefore a good idea to plan well before you even begin.

Intake - New client processing

Before you have your first appointment with a client, you will need to ensure that you can provide appropriate services to match the person's needs. Following are important questions to ask when the prospect initially contacts your office:

1. Who referred you and why? This will help to determine the type of services that are needed and identify if there is a third-party who will be paying the fees.

2. Have you had previous appointments in this office? If so, you will be able to reactivate an archived file and review the case before the client arrives for the first appointment.

3. Why do you want to see a psychologist? Gathering this information will allow you to understand the issues to be dealt with and then refer the client elsewhere if the work falls outside of your competency or mandate.

4. Who will be attending the sessions? This question provides you with an opportunity to accurately determine fees and also give an opening for discussion of confidentiality.

5. Is there any fee coverage available? You will then be able to describe the process for the client regarding payment. Some companies allow the therapist to direct bill whereas others only accept a receipt and form directly from the client who will pay you and then submit a claim. Some companies only pay a portion of the fee so the client will need to be informed about how the balance can be paid (cash, cheque, debit or credit card options should be explained).

6. What is the client contact information? You will need full name(s), address and telephone numbers.

I have a printed form which we use to record all this information. There have been several times when the receptionist neglected to complete it and if the client did not follow my twenty-four hour cancellation policy, I was unable to invoice them because I didn't have a mailing address.

Once you have gathered the above information you will need to explain:

Office location and parking.   I have all of this information as well as a map on my website so besides explaining, we give them the URL to review. Besides offering simple directions and landmarks to follow, we give specific details about what to expect such as when any outside doors may be locked and how/when they will be opened for the client.

<u>Fees and payment information</u>. Explain the fees that will be charged, when they are due and what forms of payment you accept.

<u>Cancellation policies</u>. For example, I charge the full fee if the client does not cancel or rebook twenty-four hours in advance. Messages left on the voice mail are accepted.

<u>How to access information</u> before their appointment (website, current newspaper articles or any other resources that might be helpful for them).

During the initial contact with your prospect, you will be developing rapport with them. It is a scary thing for some people to call a professional for an appointment, especially if they think that their problem is embarrassing. Your tone and words will help them to relax and look forward to their first appointment.

Setting up a new client file

Once your prospect has asked for an appointment and you have gathered the necessary information, there are some administrative tasks you need to complete as follows:

Enter the appointment in your computer calendar or appointment book.

By entering the full name(s) as well as their telephone number you will be able to contact the client without looking in a manual file if you need to do so before their appointment. I also like to enter the method of payment for the fees (Employee Assistance Company, Self or other details).

Assign a file number.

Files need to be kept for a number of years to comply with income tax rules and professional standards. I have set up a system to help with that. Each client has a unique number that consists of the year, month and number of new client referrals received in that year. The seventh new client in 2010 who calls me in May would therefore have the file number 10-05-07. I have a Word document set up where I keep track of all the file numbers that is similar to the following:

REFERRAL SOURCE	YEAR	MONTH	REFERRALS THIS YEAR	SURNAME	FIRST NAME
SELF	10	10	159	SMITH	Mary
BLUE CROSS	10	10	160	JONES	Jeff/Sue
JUSTICE	10	11	161	BROWN GREEN	Bill Belle

Prepare a file folder.

All of my client files are burgundy in colour so they are easy to identify. I use a white file label with three lines of print: Name (surname in capitals, comma and then first name), client file number and then name of payee (company, insurance or the word "Self") For example:

SMITH, Mary
10-10-159
SELF

Set up file.

I use self-sticking two-hole fasteners to hold the paperwork in the folder so there is little chance of it falling out or being misplaced.

The right-hand side has the fastener centered near the fold in a vertical position and holds referral information, reports from others sources and my handwritten notes with the most current on top.

The left-hand side which has the fastener centered at the top in a horizontal position secures financial information with a summary sheet on top that lists all the appointments and fees to date.

DATE	CLIENT	TIME	FEE	TOTAL	AMOUNT PAID	DATE	DOC #
Oct 6/10	Mary	1.25	$200	$250	$250	Oct 6/10	356 Sales Receipt
Nov 3/10	Mary/Joe	1	$300	$300			370 Invoice

Enter the information into the computer bookkeeping system.

My Quick Books system allows me to enter a "New Customer" and then "Add Job" as many times as necessary. I usually enter the company or individual who is paying the fees as the Customer. Under that I "Add Job" for the name of the client (surname, first name and the client ID number) and "Add Job" again under that for my client file number.

For example:

REGIONAL JUSTICE SERVICES
   White, John and Meg #12087
     10-10-170

File the folder in a cabinet for active clients.

Once you have completed the above, you are ready for the first appointment. There are many times, however, that the client will call to change the appointment time or provide other information. We record every single contact on a separate Contact form and immediately hole-punch and put in this in the file. This way you have all the current information but never have a pile of unfiled notes that can easily be misplaced.

Contracting as a service provider

There are several advantages to providing contracted services for organizations as follows:

1. You will have a steady stream of referrals from the company with whom you have the contract

2. You will likely be paid on a regular basis so can count on the income if your contract is with a reputable company that has good systems and practices

3. Long-term relationships with the companies can be established

The disadvantages of contracting your services are:

1. Most insurers pay a set fee per hour for the client which might be lower than your regular fee. Many do not allow you to charge the difference between their fee and your regular fee to the client so you will be working for less per hour than you might by taking on other clients.

2. You may need to complete specific forms required by the company.

3. Payment is usually done on a monthly basis and may be one to several months after the services were provided.

There are several different types of contracts that can be negotiated in your private practise. In order to incorporate them into your business you will need to ensure that you understand the options and details of each contract.

1. **Government programs** - Before you are placed on a "provider" list you may have to go through a rather extensive process where you are required to provide your credentials and/or references. Government departments usually have a set fee schedule and payment procedures which are rigid. Usually you are advised of the number of sessions that have been approved at the time of the client referral.

2. **Employee Assistance Programs** - These are usually benefit plans that have been arranged by the client's employer who pays an insurance company for services on behalf of the client. It is "use it or lose it" for the client who cannot carry unused hours over into the next insured year. Most of these programs are short-term and designed to assess the client who is then referred to community

resources. You invoice the insurer for their set fee and wait for payment based on their terms.

3.   **Health Spending Accounts** - Many employers have been providing clients with this type of benefit rather than giving them a defined benefit plan. The client can choose how to use the account balance for a number of eligible services such as vision, dental or health care. You are paid your regular fee and the client submits the receipt you provide to their plan for reimbursement.

4.   **Insurance Plans** - Some companies purchase insurance packages which have several aspects to them including short-term disability and long-term disability benefits. Therapy services usually are limited and may be restricted to those provided by a psychologist. If the employee is on a leave from work, s/he may have a designated worker who will negotiate a block of hours for the client to work with you on specific goals. These will then be directly billed to the worker and are paid for by the insurer.

7.   **Supplemented programs** - Many companies will provide a limited number of sessions with a defined hourly fee but allow you to invoice the client for the difference between those fees and what you would otherwise charge. You will therefore need to create two invoices - one for the company and one for the client (top up), each with the appropriate amounts that total your full hourly rate.

8.   **Self-referrals** - Some clients do not have any coverage and pay the entire fee after each appointment. I recommend that they provide the receipts to their accountant who will determine if they can claim them under "Medical Expenses" on their income tax annual submission.

Contracting with different types of programs can provide balance for your business. At the same time, however, you will be required to decide if you want to accommodate being paid lower fees and accepting the company's invoicing procedures and payment terms. Be sure that you enter into each contract with all of the information necessary so that you won't feel disappointed or resentful at a later date.

File administration

One of the most important aspects of providing service to clients is to ensure that proper and complete documentation is done. Besides promoting efficiency in your business and being able to trace the work you have done with and for the client, you may need to produce information at a later date for government audit, Court cases, to resolve complaints or to measure progress.

Each contact you have with the client, whether it is by telephone, email or in person, must be recorded with the date, name of the individuals involved, information shared and plan of action for the future. I have developed a form with four sections:

1. How/why the person made contact

2. Billing information (date, name of individual, time used during the contact, rate per hour, total fee for the contact, organization or person responsible for fees).

3. Blank lines where I can write details of the contact. I always try to write in such a simple and clear manner that a child could read what I wrote and understand it.

4. Action steps for dealing with this (file, request file extension, return call, provide referral)

All information, reports and notes are put into a file that is labeled for the particular client and stored in a locked cabinet in a secure setting.

When the contact consists of billable time, I immediately invoice the appropriate source, print the invoice, file it on the left-hand side of the file and record the invoice on the summary sheet which I keep at the top of that side of the file.

Dr. Linda Hancock Inc.   Page _____

Existing File ___   New File ___   New Referral ____   E-mail____
Telephone ___   Voice Mail ___   Face-to-Face ___   Case Conference ___

CLIENT (S): _____

OTHER (S): _____

DATE: _____   TIME: _____ to _____

BILLING: _____(HR) x \$_____ = _____   Paid ____   Invoice ___

CONTRACT: _____

_____
_____
_____
_____
_____
_____
_____
_____
_____

File ___   Invoice ___   Write Report ___   Extension ___   Send Letter/Notes ___

Special Instructions: _____

When reports are received from other professionals or organizations, I file them on the right-hand side of the file under a colored sheet of paper that separates them from my file notes which are filed chronologically on top of them.

All information from other sources is confidential and should not be shared with the client or with other sources without the written permission of the individual who prepared the report.

When services have been completed and the balance of the account has been paid in full, I remove the file from the active drawer and complete a file closure summary sheet that includes the client names, file numbers, reason for closure, number of sessions, reason and source of original referral, special comments and my signature.

This form is secured on the right-hand side of the file which is then moved to the storage for inactive files. Remember to also move the customer file in your computer bookkeeping system to inactive status.

Dr. Linda Hancock Inc.

FILE CLOSURE FORM

Client: _____ File #: _____

Client: _____ File #: _____

Date: _____

Reason for Closure:
___ Goals met
___ Funding ended
___ Moved
___ Client Withdrew from Services
___ Mutual Agreement
___ Referral made to: _____
___ Other

Date file was opened: _____

Referred by: _____

For: _____

Number of sessions: _____

Last session: _____

Comments:
_____
_____

_____
Dr. Linda Hancock, BA, BSW, M.Ed., PSY.D.
Registered Psychologist and Registered Social Worker

Dr. Linda Hancock

Never release any information from the file to anyone unless you have written informed consent from the client or a legal subpoena. In either case, consulting with a practice adviser or your regulatory body will likely be helpful in determining what and how to release information. It is usually done on a "need to know" basis.

Confidentiality also involves never leaving a file in any place where it might be seen by others. Even if a person only reads the file label, this is a confidentiality breach.

It is best to not remove paper files from your office to ensure that they will not be misplaced or lost. But even in the office when they are locked in cabinets and rooms, there is a chance that they will be lost or destroyed if there is a fire or water damage in the building.

My older son who operates a successful computer business has encouraged me to value electronic file storage. He set up an inexpensive portable hard drive that backs up my office computer automatically every night. Because it can easily be carried in a briefcase, I am able to take it with me and therefore have all my electronic files in two locations. A third protection is that we can also access the files through the server he owns in the case of an emergency.

Backing up files, whether it is done on a disc, memory stick, or hard drive might take a few minutes but will save you days or weeks of work should there be a problem with your computer or damage to your physical office.

Communicating with staff and contracted workers

If you are going to be working with someone, it is important that you have clear communication, common goals, deadlines for completing tasks and a relationship that promotes harmony. Without these, you will find that resentment builds and the work doesn't get done on time or in an appropriate manner!

There are a number of things you can do to ensure that you and your staff or contract personnel have the best possible working relationship:

Know Exactly What You Need - Before you hire someone or sign a contract, know exactly what you want the other person to do for you. Make a list of all the tasks and timeframes for their completion. It is important to not only give the other person your expectations in writing but also to review these verbally so there are no misunderstandings. Also consider whether you will be paying the person through a regular salary or with an hourly contracted rate for each project.

Don't Assume Anything -. People cannot read your mind and not everyone thinks the same so assuming that they know what you want will just result in problems.

I remember when I first started hiring staff. I assumed that they had the skills and passion to do the job the way I wanted things to be done. I was wrong - repeatedly! Finally I figured it out!

Be Prepared to Monitor and Evaluate -.Plan regular times to review progress with the person who you have assigned to complete tasks and projects. Asking "How are things going?" is not necessarily going to give you the information that you need (or want). Set a regular time each day or week to talk. Ask good questions and take the time to make sure that progress is being made as agreed upon.

Remember that the buck stops with you -. Even though it is important to encourage the staff and provide a spirit of forgiveness for errors, those who cannot or do not meet the standards or deadlines laid out, will jeopardize your reputation and financial situation. Be honest with the other person. If you don't like what is happening, discuss this openly and develop ways of improving the situation.

Remember, it is up to you to protect yourself. If someone cannot do the job, don't repeatedly ignore the mistakes or put up with shoddy work. Find someone who can do the work and hire them!

Running a business is about building profit and security by offering excellent services. This will occur only when you and your staff or contracted workers are able to communicate effectively with each other and get things done in a timely manner.

Setting up a system to handle information overload

"I am not disorganized — I know *exactly* where everything is! The newer stuff is on top and the older stuff is on the bottom."

My adult children were disgusted when they noticed that I had several hundred emails in my Inbox and couldn't find anything with ease. They become even more annoyed, however, when I print documents that they think could have been better left as digital records.

You see, they have grown up with computers and therefore have learned how to deal with things in a different way than I have. They also are used to protecting the environment and trusting electronic files whereas I tend to feel more comfortable with physical files and printed documents.

Because we live in a world in which we receive an overwhelming amount of information, it is important to learn how to manage it in an effective manner. Following are some tips for handling both electronic and printed data:

1. **Set up folders** in your email software to hold information that needs to be kept. I tend to use the name of the person who sent it to me and the folder name but you can use any method that will help you to file and then find it again.

2. **Deal with things as they arrive**. Organizational specialists recommend that you only touch a piece of paper once. Your choices are act on it, file it, or destroy it. The same applies to emails.

3. **Develop a system for storing paper reports** or documents that you need to keep. It only takes a couple of minutes to properly label a file folder. You might find that scanning the item into the computer is even more effective than storing the physical copy.

4. **Ensure that all of your photos are downloaded** from your camera and labeled properly. It is easier to do this as you take photos rather than wait until you have hundreds of photos to organize.

5. **Learn about specific techniques that you can use to search** for information stored on your hard drive. Perhaps you might take a computer course or spend time with a teen who is an avid computer user.

6. **Get rid of everything you don't need**. If you can't name the items in a box before opening it, you likely don't need them. Shred and destroy!

7. **Keep your voice mailbox cleared**. Writing a list of caller names and numbers will allow you to delete the messages as you listen to them. It looks very unprofessional when a client calls your office and is informed that they cannot leave a message because your mailbox is full.

Dr. Linda Hancock

Managing information involves having a plan that includes responding to it, filing it or destroying it.

- Responding means you will deal with it right away.
- Filing means that you will have an efficient system which will allow you to quickly find it again when it is needed.
- Destroying it means that you have a shredder, garbage can and trash folder available for immediate use.

Tasks checklist

Certain tasks need to be done on daily, weekly, monthly, quarterly and yearly schedules. Have a list of things that you need to do on a regular basis and then ensure that you do them according to the time frames listed. The reward is that when you reach the end of the year everything is done!

Habits can be formed in a matter of weeks and it is therefore important that you plan and develop specific checks and balances so that good habits are formed in your business.

Following is a listing of things that I do on a regular basis as part of my SUCCESS system.

Daily:

Complete all your paperwork - it is easier to do this when thoughts are fresh in your mind and less stressful than facing a desk full of things that need to be finished.

1. Answer and return all telephone calls. If you are really stretched for time, mark the ones that can wait in an available slot on the calendar. Remember to include the telephone number and a brief description of the topic to be discussed.
2. Open all mail and sort into piles by category (accounts receivables, payables, reading, general correspondence).

3. Enter any bills that are received that day and print cheques for dates that are as close as possible to the date that they are due. Store them with a sticky note that specifies the date they should be mailed in order to reach the vendor before the due date and thus save being charged interest.

4. Throughout the day, keep a list of things that you need to do or ensure that they are marked on your calendar so they will be completed by the expected date. This will allow you to clear your mind without worry about forgetting things.

5. See the clients who are booked for the day and provide receipts to those who pay their fees themselves. Remember to schedule another appointment with them!

6. Complete the entire contract invoicing for that day's work. The sooner you mail, email or FAX them - the sooner you will be paid for your work

7. Enter the invoiced time and fees charged beside each client's name in your calendar. Also enter times and amounts for billable reports which you completed. Then print out the daily calendar page.

8. Print a copy of the day's sales report from your computer bookkeeping program, compare it to the amounts invoiced on your daily calendar page and file both sheets together for future reference in a folder labeled with the name of the month.

9. Complete all filing. Try to do this throughout the day between clients so that you don't have a stack of it at the end of the day when you are ready to leave the office. Make a commitment to only touch a piece of paper once and you will soon find that completing a task and immediately filing the document is a valuable and time-saving habit.

10. Record payments you received on account in the computer. Prepare the bank deposit and take it to the bank at the end of the day. Having a debit card will allow you to make deposits in the ATM after banking hours without incurring any extra costs for using a night depository.

Cash flow is very important, especially when you are just beginning your business, and having regular deposits will help you to develop a good reputation with your bank.

11. Walk through the office before you leave and quickly put things in order so that the next day you are ready to welcome clients.

12 Take any outgoing mail to the post office or drop box. It is easy to procrastinate but I find that no matter how late it is when I leave the office, it is better to do this on the date that the mail was prepared.

Weekly

1. Submit invoices and any reports required by contracted agencies. (Some companies will not accept billing except on the dates that they specify).
2. Order any supplies that are needed
3. Review your week to determine if you have met your goals.
4. Quickly scan the calendar for the following week so you can mentally prepare for what is scheduled.
5. Ensure that a thorough cleaning of the office is done (either by you or a janitor). Depending on the size of your office and the amount of traffic, you might find that hiring a service is an affordable option.

Monthly

1. Send out statements for accounts with balances and ensure that all work has been invoiced for contract agencies that require submission of month-end forms
2. Review Accounts Receivable list and contact overdue accounts to arrange payment.
3. Prepare and submit any payroll remittances (if applicable) and any required government reports or submissions.
4. Ensure that you have paid all business bills for the month including your rent or lease payment (you may have scheduled these for specific dates through Internet banking or have written cheques to be mailed on specific dates).
5. Reconcile bank and credit card statements

6. Print monthly reports.
7. Review Monthly Sales Report, Last Year Comparison Report, Profit and Loss Report from your computer program to see how your business is doing.
8. Close client files that have been inactive for 90 days.

Quarterly

1. Complete any government or tax submission reports
2. Touch base with accountant to review business progress
3. Review quarterly reports on the computer and set goals for next quarter

Yearly

1. Submit electronic and paper records to the accountant for preparation of income tax Return and Financial Statements.
2. Prepare Business Plan for next year (It is best to do this in October so it is ready for the beginning of the new year. I actually prefer to write two-year plans).
3. Review client list and thank them for working with you.
4. Celebrate your business accomplishments!

So many times I hear professionals argue that seeing the client is the most important part of the business and therefore should have first priority. Because paperwork can be boring they often procrastinate and do it only when it is absolutely necessary. The result is that they are often frustrated and scrambling to find information that they need.

A tax audit puts them in serious distress!

If you set up a simple but efficient system and follow the steps regularly you will soon find that you have less stress, more knowledge and control over your business and the confidence to know that even a tax audit will be done with the least amount of effort.

My accountant attests to the fact that those who have things in order have fewer problems with auditors and investigators. You see, an organized system reduces the stress for them and allows them to do their jobs quickly and with fewer difficulties.

And – a happy tax man is more willing to give you the benefit of the doubt!

Also, by having a good system in place you will find that your workload is distributed throughout the year and you won't ever have to face a time when you feel unprepared or a year end that is overwhelming!

Networking

You and your clients will benefit from developing relationships with professionals in the community and ensuring that you know the proper procedure for completing an appropriate referral. One of the things that I have learned over the years is to value the services and support offered by other organizations and businesses.

Networking with other business owners, community resources and professionals will benefit you in a number of ways.

1. Expanding your knowledge -. Our world is constantly changing and it is impossible to keep up with everything but developing relationships with people who work in various careers will provide ongoing discussion opportunities and a resource base where you can have specific questions answered. You will always be on the cutting edge for new information
2. Participating on collaborative teams - Often solutions to problems can be best handled by individuals who form alliances. Whether it is to deal with systemic policies or individual client problems, a team often is able to present creative and personalized solutions that might not otherwise be available.
3. Developing extensive referral resources - Learning about the mandates and referral processes for other resources, will allow you to ensure that your clients' needs can be met when you feel you do not have the competency required to meet them yourself. Financial planners, lawyers, psychiatrists, or inpatient addiction

programs all have specific referral procedures. Knowing the people involved will help you to understand these and allow you to assist your client through the transition process.

4. <u>Enjoying Support</u> - Everyone needs to have individuals in their life who understand the work you do and care about your well-being, especially when it is very demanding. It also can be very comforting to know that someone is available to offer you helpful advice for a specific situation.

Over the years, I have been so thankful to have built relationships with people who encourage me in my career and support me when I'm tired or unsure about something.

Professionals that start with the letter "P"

Sometimes I tell my clients that it is important that they have three people in their lives who can work together to help them with their health challenges. All three start with the letter "P".

Physicians are medical doctors who have been trained primarily to look after your body. They usually have hospital privileges and clinical appointment times which allow interview, examination and specific testing to determine illness. After assessments are completed, doctors then treat the "patients" usually with medications. We all know how busy doctors can be and I have noticed signs in some of their offices informing patients that due to time restrictions, only one problem will be dealt with at a visit.

It is interesting to note that a large percentage of individuals who visit their doctor either don't have a physical ailment or are ill because of a mental or emotional problem. Relationship difficulties, grief, depression, anxiety or other psychological problems can result in a visit to the doctor even if the problem might be treated better in another setting.

Psychiatrists are medical doctors who have specialized in the field of thought and mood disorders. Some have hospital privileges which they use for testing or admitting purposes. Many operate businesses in private clinics. They focus on assessment and treatment of individuals who may be suffering from a wide range of mental illnesses that include schizophrenia, sleep disorders, various types of depression, or other diagnoses most often referred to in the *Diagnostic and Statistical Manual (DSM-IV-TR)* published by the *American Psychiatric Association*. Most often an assessment consists of an interview with the psychiatrist who then offers a number of treatment options including medication for the "patient" with follow-up appointments to assess their effectiveness.

Psychologists are professionals who study how people think, feel and behave from a scientific viewpoint. They then apply the knowledge to help people understand, explain and change their behaviours and develop healthier patterns. This is done through assessment, consultation or treatment in specific areas of focus such as Industrial/Organizational, Clinical, Forensic, Educational, or Research Psychology. Psychologists may work in any of these specific settings or operate a private psychology practice where "clients" book and attend appointments. Psychologists do not usually have prescription or hospitalization privileges but instead focus on providing "talk therapy" to help their "clients" with difficulties.

Physicians, psychiatrists and psychologists have more than six years of formal post-secondary training as well as internships before they practice independently. They are each licensed through regulatory bodies which have a *Code of Ethics* and *Standards of Practice*. They all use science as a foundation to their work.

What differentiates them is how they help others. There is some overlap, but their focus is very specific to the field in which they practice.

If you are having some physical, mental or emotional difficulties, you may benefit from having a team of professionals who will examine your situation and work together with you in order to help you to reach your maximum health potential.

Remember, you are the business and if you aren't healthy, the business will not be healthy.

Planning Your Success

- ❑ Have you set up the three necessary systems for your business?

- ❑ Does technology make your life easier?

- ❑ Do you have a good bookkeeping system?

- ❑ What types of filing systems would help you?

- ❑ Do you have a system for new clients?

- ❑ Have you set up a standardized method for new client files?

- ❑ Do you understand types and options for contracting?

- ❑ How will you communicate with staff and workers?

- ❑ Are you committed to following the task checklist?

- ❑ How will you build a good network?

- ❑ What other professionals do you need to maintain good health?

Notes:

Chapter Five

ENSURING YOUR PRACTICE
IS STRONG

Standards of practice and competency

It is one thing to think that you are helpful and another to actually be helpful.

Most professions have developed *Standards of Practice* which define and outline requirements for competent service. Some occupations also fall under government legislation. It is very important that you know and understand exactly what is required.

Pleading "ignorance" is not acceptable.

I don't think anyone would be foolish enough to let someone do brain surgery on them merely because the other person is interested in the brain. No matter how persuasive that person is, I am sure you would not give them a chance to practice on you! You would first want to know that they had training, experience and skills in the area of performing brain surgery.

It is the same for your clients. When they come to you for help, they want to know that you have knowledge, skills and abilities that are backed with both training and experience. They also want to know that they can be confident you will not harm them.

It is your responsibility to ensure that you know the standards of practice and follow them. If you are unsure or don't feel confident in a specific area, you can improve through various means including self-study, completing courses or workshops, setting up mentee arrangements or doing internships.

Unconscious incompetence means that you don't know what you don't know. We all have blind spots that can jeopardize our personal and professional lives. Because of these, it is important that we have honest peers who will not only point out our flaws but also help us to figure out how to overcome them.

Developing expertise will provide many benefits for you and your clients. Everyone will have more confidence and be able to trust the idea that clients will receive good ethical services to help them with their problem.

© 1999 Randy Glasbergen.   www.glasbergen.com

"The committee met to approve your idea. But first we had to approve the approval, providing everyone agreed to disagree to approve the agreement which approved the approval agreement. After that, things got complicated."

Licenses and Insurance

There are some costs of doing business that cannot be ignored without consequences. Research will allow you to ensure that you have the proper licenses and insurance to protect your business.

Licenses:

1. Professional licenses - Contact your regulatory body in order to determine exactly what annual fees and requirements are necessary in order to obtain and renew your license to practice. One of the most important things you will do each year is pay the fees in full by the date they are due so as not to jeopardize your credentials.

2. City or municipal - Each region has its own bylaws and you will therefore need to do some research to determine if or what kind of licenses are needed in order for you to open and operate your business. Certain types of therapists are classified as health professionals and therefore may be exempt from requiring city or municipal licenses. On the other hand, you may be required to pay city taxes even if you do not own the building where your office is housed. If you are unsure where to begin, contact City Hall and/ or another professional in your field to gather information.

Whatever you do, buy the required licenses. The last thing you need is a fine and loss of reputation that might result if you do not so do.

Insurance:

We never seem to notice the leak in the roof until it rains but how we wish we had purchased insurance when it does rain!

There are three types of insurance that the solo professional will need to consider purchasing:

1. **Liability** - If someone files a formal complaint or decides to sue you, your entire life will be affected. It may take months or even years to come to a resolution and the legal costs can mount

significantly. Many Employee Assistance Programs require that you have at least $2 million coverage but some demand as much as $5 million coverage. This type of insurance is not an option. You must protect yourself as a professional.

2. **Property** - A fire or flood can leave you in a very vulnerable position and actually prevent you from re-establishing your practice on a short or long-term basis depending on the costs involved. Purchasing property insurance will help you to replace items that are destroyed or damaged due to circumstances you cannot control.

3. **Life and Disability** - You and your family will likely suffer if you are ill or disabled to the point that you cannot work for a period of time. Disability insurance, however, will provide you with an income until you are well and able to return to your business. Also, if you have an appropriate amount of life insurance, your family will be protected from serious financial vulnerability that may otherwise occur upon your death.

The insurance industry is quite competitive and you might find that you can save a great deal by pricing out policies from a number of different companies. Ensure, however, that they have comparable benefits and that your final purchasing decision is not just based on price.

Before you see the new client

As a solo professional you will likely not be paid until you actually meet with your new client. There are several things that you need to do in order to ensure that the first meeting happens.

1. Offer a friendly and professional first impression. Many clients decide whether they will meet with you based on their initial contact with your office.

2. Ensure the client is a good match - You will need a brief understanding of their problem in order to determine if you are competent to help that person. If the client believes that you can

help the chances that the person will show up for the appointment increase.

3. Clearly inform the client about things that you will not do for them - If they are asking you to do things that are outside your mandate or ethical boundaries, it is important that s/he knows that before the first appointment. It also leaves the appointment time open for someone else.

4. Give directions to your office - When a client is lost or late for an appointment it may affect not only your first appointment, but also your future relationship. Give a clear description of how to arrive at your office and landmarks which will help the person to find it.

5. Determine how and when your fees will be paid. It is easier for both of you to discuss this before the first appointment so that necessary calls for insurance approval or other arrangements can be made.

6. Obtain necessary consents and other paperwork. If you are seeing children, for example, you will need to have signatures of informed consent from both parents. Paperwork from referral sources should also be requested and received before the first appointment.

7. Follow up on appointments that are cancelled. If the client decided not to attend because of something you can correct in the future, it is important that you know that so you can make an adjustment for future growth. On the other hand, most people cancel their appointments because of personal issues. Your follow up call may be exactly what they need at the time and will likely encourage them to rebook with you.

8. Complete your administrative process. Prepare a file and enter your information into your accounting system. You will not only be more organized, but also have less stress knowing that everything is in order so that you can spend the least amount of time during the appointment on these tasks.

If you take extra care at the beginning of a business relationship, you will earn the respect of your client and eliminate problems that may interfere with getting off to a good start with them. Just think about how you would like to be treated and then offer that same type of quality service to your client.

What is informed consent?

I recently heard the sad story of a woman who woke up from an investigative surgery to find to her horror that one of her breasts was missing. She had obviously signed consent for the hospital and doctor to do the surgery but did not have enough information to know what the results of that might be. She gave consent but, because she didn't totally understand, it could be said that she didn't give informed consent.

Sometimes we give permission, approval or agreement to something but don't have enough information to understand the process that will be used or the risks associated with it.

Have you ever taken your car to a mechanic to find out why it wasn't working properly and when you returned to pick it up were presented with a large and unexpected invoice? I bet you were angry for not being consulted before the work was done. If you had known why the vehicle was not working properly you might have asked about the possibility of getting used parts or leaving the repairs to a later date.

It is important that you gather information from your client, explain their options and let them make decisions about how they want to proceed.

When you agree to have your child assessed by a psychologist do you know what tests will be used, what they are measuring or how the results may affect your child's placement in the school system? Will there be a report? Who will get copies of it? Will someone explain it to you? You and your clients need a great deal of information before you can actually give informed consent.

I once heard about parents who were upset when they discovered that their child had been given an IQ test. They didn't understand that this is one of the outcomes of a *Weschler Intelligence Scale for Children (WISC)*. Even though they had agreed to use this test, they didn't understand the full implications of what the testing would provide. They had given consent but really hadn't had enough information to call it informed consent.

Assessments for Court purposes can also be confusing and upsetting if the parties do not have full understanding. Often individuals who are going through divorce, for example, think that they can hire a psychologist to state that they would be the best parent for the children and therefore should have sole custody. It is easy to assume that paying for a professional will guarantee support for one's case. Psychologists who are involved in custody and access cases focus on the needs of the children and not merely on the parent who has paid for the report so the parent who had specific expectations might be very disappointed with the results.

Informed Consent means that you know in advance what services will be provided, how they will be conducted and the possible outcomes. Treatment for depression, for example, can consist of Cognitive-Behavioural therapy, hypnotism, medication, or a number of other therapies. Make sure whether you are the client or the professional involved that it is clear which treatment will be used, how often and for what duration.

Speak clearly about your professional qualifications, confidentiality, report writing and release of information. Explain any risks that might be involved.

The whole area of fees can also be confusing and should be a part of the informed consent process. How much will you charge for your services? When is payment to be made? Are there options or insurance coverage that might help with this?

Informed Consent is designed to protect you and your client. Being a wise consumer means asking questions and ensuring that you understand what will happen, how, when, where and the risks that you face. As a professional it also means that you help your client to understanding clearly what they are agreeing to do.

Don't have your clients consent to do anything that they don't understand fully. They may end up being horribly disappointed, upset or even changed for life in a way that you or they wouldn't have chosen! And, when you client is upset you are risk as they may decide to file a formal complaint against you with your regulatory body.

Outlining limits to confidentiality

Most people think that confidentiality means that what everything they say will be protected without exception. Verbal information and written records about a client cannot be shared with another party without the written consent of the client or the client's legal guardian, however, therapists are also required to comply with provincial and federal privacy legislation in the collection and retention of personal information.

Before any services are provided it is therefore important that you review with the client all of the exclusions outlined in legislation that form limits to confidentiality.

Provinces, states and federal laws differ regarding exceptions to confidentiality and/or privacy. Following are the clauses that I have in my Consultation Agreement which reflect Alberta legislation:

> **Suicide or homicide** *(Duty to Warn and Protect):* If you disclose the intent or a plan to harm another person, I am required to warn the intended victim and report this information to legal authorities. In cases in which you disclose or imply a plan for suicide, I am required to notify legal authorities and make reasonable attempts to ensure your safety.

> **Abuse** (of Children or Vulnerable Adult). If you state that you have recently, are presently or are in danger of abusing a child or vulnerable adult, I am required to report this information to Child Protective Services and/or the Police.

> **Legal matters** *within the Justice System.* If you are in trouble with the law or have matters before a judge I may be served with a

Court Order to appear as a fact or expert witness or to release your records to the Courts or their representatives.

Subpoena of your file If I receive a Court document such as a subpoena, I am required to release your records as indicated.

Requests to share information with others (*Release of Information*). If you and I agree that I will speak with or for you with another individual (or individuals) on your behalf to further the ultimate goals of the referral information we will add the names of those individuals to this agreement. This confirms your permission for me to use verbal or written communication through conversation with the individuals named or by preparing and/or sending reports to the individual.

Information Required by a Coroner or Medical Examiner's Office

Informed consent means that your client clearly understands the limits to confidentiality and agrees to proceed knowing them.

The importance of documentation

When you are in business you will need to have a system for documentation that results in accurate files and, at the same time, frees up your memory to perform important tasks.

Following are some tips to help you with your documentation:

1. Document every single contact you have with clients and other professionals - This sounds like a lot of work but is not nearly as difficult as trying to remember when you talked with someone-especially if you are to appear in a Court hearing or before a review panel.

2. Prepare a template that is easy to use for any type of contact. - The form that I use is multi-purpose and not only has the name(s) of the individual(s) involved, date, time, billing fee and applicable contract, but also has lines on two-thirds of the page for hand-

written notes. I keep blank copies on clipboards that are placed in spots around the office so they are easy to access when there is telephone or personal interaction. (See a sample of my template under "File Administration").

3. Write like a ten-year-old will be reading the notes - Make sure that everything you write down is detailed and understandable to others beside yourself. It is amazing how quickly you can forget what happened during contacts with others but having clear and complete notes will help you to remember. Your notes must be written in a simple and clear manner so that anyone could pick up the file and understand details of your conversation.

4. Write notes within 24 hours of contact - I made a rule for myself several years ago that I would not leave the office at night until all my notes were completed. There are several benefits to doing this including the fact that you can then have an evening without the stress of thinking that there is paperwork piling up for you. Also, if you are called to Court, your diligence will be honoured as most Courts recognize the fact that if you write things down within 24 hours, your memory will be more accurate than leaving the notes until later. Report writing is also much easier if you have detailed notes to review.

    I once went on vacation and was shocked to return to the office to find that one of the children on my caseload had died while I was away. My file had immediately been taken for investigative purposes and I was so thankful that I had left everything in order.

5. File your notes immediately - When you have piles of papers on your desk, you can experience unnecessary stress, whereas a file that is complete and in order will help you to let go and focus on other activities. Filing your notes may only take a few seconds while piling them up may cause hours of work for a later date.

Many therapists state that people are the most important part of the job and leave their paperwork until they are either in trouble with an employer or so totally overwhelmed and disorganized that they have a huge investment of time to put things in order. Paperwork is just as important (or more so at times) than working with the client.

Doing your documentation on a daily basis is a habit to be developed which offers huge rewards. It helps you to keep things in order and gives you confidence that you have accurate notes of what occurred. It also protects you from being a victim of memory loss or being accused of incompetency.

Building a wonderful reputation

One of the lawyers in our city once said "It takes a lifetime to build a reputation and a second to lose it". People are attracted to businesses and professionals who have good reputations and it is therefore important that you focus on building and maintaining one that is admirable.

It is difficult, if not impossible, to separate the values, practices and integrity of the business from those of the individuals who operate the business - especially in the case of solo professionals. You are the business and your actions, whether they are in your personal or professional practice, are being observed and judged by your peers and clients.

It never ceases to amaze me when people say one thing and do another thinking that the discrepancy will not catch up to them. Inevitably, the preacher who delivers sermons on "sins of the flesh" will be found out for sexual improprieties. Those who at first appear to be successful in advising others regarding their financial portfolios, often end up in jail for embezzlement. Even sports and film role-models can lose the respect of fans when they are caught with illegal drug use or criminal behaviours.

Aren't you disappointed when you find out that one of the individuals, who you respected, has not measured up to your expectations?

It is not enough to carry on with inappropriate choices and then think you can merely ask forgiveness and carry on without consequences.

Dr. Linda Hancock

Building and maintaining a good reputation involves adopting good values and practices in both personal and professional arenas. Offering good services, resolving problems in a healthy and fair manner while role-modeling compassion and good skills will help you to build an admired reputation that will extend well beyond your community.

Think for a moment of the people in your life who you would name as having your respect and trust. Is your own name on that list? Would you describe yourself as having a good reputation?

Remember, even if you do have a good reputation now, it can be lost in a second. Protect it by continuing to make good choices because, as a solo professional your reputation is one of your very best assets.

Taking care of your personal and professional needs

As solo professionals, we often have problems and therefore need to know who and where to get help for ourselves. It is important to develop a network of individuals who you can consult with for both personal and professional issues.

Family and Friends - I always advise my clients to let their family be their family and their friends be their friends. Expecting those who are close to you to become your financial advisor, therapist or parenting resource can cause problems and actually hurt the relationship you have with them. They likely do not have the training or objectivity that you would get from working with a professional.

Families and friendships have different types of boundaries and styles. Be cautious when you are seeking help from these sources. An individual may give you bad advice, make suggestions that you are not prepared to follow or even try to solve the problem in a controlling manner. And remember - you can't fire your mother-in-law!

You can offer and receive support from family and friends if you wish, but be very careful about what you share with them! They will

142

remember what you said and may remind you for years to come of things that you just want to put in the past.

It's wonderful to be part of a warm and caring family. Just be careful about what type of support you ask for as you may live with regret having shared too much information that might better have been dealt with in a different way.

Professional help for personal issues - You cannot be a competent professional if you have untreated issues such as addictions, relationship problems or mental illness. Loss, hurt or stress can interfere with you being able to live well and work competently. It is a good idea to be honest about your problems and then seek appropriate competent services to help you deal with them.

I have a client who once told me "Everyone needs a therapist". Find someone who you can trust to help you deal with things that might otherwise interfere with your ability to perform up to your potential.

Professional Support - Over the years I have been able to build good relationships with individuals who work in the areas of psychology and social work. They have taught me so much about ways to improve my practice and are very willing consultants who I can access when needed. The professionals who work with similar clients to yours understand better than anyone else and won't be shocked or ignorant about any problems or circumstances that you might bring to them.

Your regulatory body can also provide information, educational opportunities or practice advisors for specific issues.

Besides this, it is important to widen your circle to include other business people and professionals. Their perspectives might be exactly what you need to understand the trends and dynamics that are affecting society and having an impact on your clients.

Organizations and Internet sites -When you feel that you are lacking knowledge about a specific topic, you can usually find an organization that has the exact information you need. For example, my sister has

Multiple Sclerosis and when she had a problem with itching skin we contacted the *MS Society* for advice. Within 24 hours she was called by an expert and began taking the appropriate medication to resolve the itching.

Most organizations have websites that offer articles on common themes and contact information for resources.

Begin developing support networks in all of the above areas and expand them over time. You will soon find that strong bonds of trust and relationship will help you to grow both personally and professionally.

Five important things to do every day

The world has so many distractions and it is very easy to become overwhelmed with them rather than focusing on the things that will keep your business strong. There are five specific tasks that will help you to stay on track if they are done every day. Each takes only a few minutes but will bring you definite rewards.

1. **Return all client telephone calls and contacts** - Even leaving an interesting voice mail message is better than ignoring clients. Rather than merely stating "I am returning your call", say something that will save time or be helpful for the client. For example, "I received your request for an appointment and have openings on Tuesday at 2 pm and Thursday at 9 am. I will tentatively mark you in for both and look forward to receiving a message today with your choice. Don't worry. If neither works for you, we will find one that does."

2. **Make your bank deposit** - No matter how much you enjoy your work, the bottom line is to have profit and develop a good credit history. Making a deposit each day, even if it is small, can save you interest charged on your business line of credit and demonstrates to your bank that you have regular income. Remember, this is YOUR financial health and YOUR reputation that you are building.

3. **Complete your file notes** - It is far easier to remember what you and your client did before the day ends than it is after time passes. Documenting not only helps you feel a sense of organization but also prevents you from facing embarrassment if your file is called into Court or your cases are reviewed by your professional body or contracting organization.

4. **Tidy your work area** - Quickly cleaning off your desk, putting files away and ensuring that things are neat will give you and your clients a "fresh start" the following day. It is very difficult to walk into a room that looks like a bomb went off. Putting things away properly ensures confidentiality and gives everyone the impression that you are organized. Your work area is a reflection of you and your values.

5. **Do one thing to expand your business** - Marketing can easily get lost in busy days. Whether it is calling a referral source, researching a networking group or even tweeting a 140 character message, you will need to reach out to others. Files will close over time and if you do not have new clients, your business will die. Be creative and consistent in your promotional activities.

It is true that little things do make a difference. You will likely never get everything done in a day but adopting some good habits will help you to focus on the most important things. And it won't take long until you develop the sense of confidence that comes with having an established routine.

Stay focused

Often clients ask me how they can keep up with all the demands in their lives. Usually they are feeling overwhelmed because they are doing things that could be done by someone else - either family members, staff or contracted workers.

Imagine that each person has a business circle and within that circle are three or four things that only that person can do. In my business, for example, I am the only person who is licensed to see the clients, able to write the books that share my perspective and contracted to do the speaking presentations. I therefore focus on doing therapy, writing and speaking. Everything else is outside my circle and could therefore be done by someone else. I can hire someone to do the janitorial work, answer telephones or work at a book table.

When I work within my circle, I do well, feel good and earn a decent income. On the other hand, when I am outside of the circle, I tend to get distracted from my purpose. This can result in frustration and financial stress.

If you are feeling overwhelmed, it is time to consider the tasks you are facing and decide whether they even need to be done and, if so, by whom.

Stop right now and in the circle below write the three or four business tasks that only you can do?

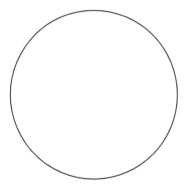

Now just because you CAN do something doesn't mean that you SHOULD be doing it. I can do a newsletter, for example, but not to the caliber or in the same amount of time as someone who has expertise in this field. I become frustrated quickly when looking for graphics whereas my son enjoys coming up with appropriate design and in mere seconds can produce beautiful work that I might struggle with for hours. You need skills, equipment and time to produce professional quality and sometimes I am lacking in one or all of these areas.

Open for Business Success

There are times when you can waste time and end up with inferior results on projects that could be done by someone who is gifted and would do them quite inexpensively. Even if you enjoy doing some things, you need to consider whether doing them builds your business better than if you were doing one of the three or four things in your circle.

Perhaps there are some things that you have been doing over and over and over again. Many professionals make the mistake of not researching options or teaching others how to do tedious tasks. They think that it is "easier to do it" themselves the way they have always been doing them.

Evaluate the things you do repeatedly that are annoying you. Perhaps teaching someone once or setting up a computer system to streamline the project would be a better investment of your time.

Now, let's invest some time in planning. Make a chart like the one below and enter all the tasks that you are doing.

TASK	DOES IT NEED TO BE DONE?	IS THIS IN MY CIRCLE?	CAN I TEACH SOMEONE OR AUTOMATE IT?	WHO CAN I GET TO DO THIS?

Schedule a regular but limited block of time to work on the tasks in the fourth column. You might think that you cannot afford to hire people to do the identified work but, consider that you might actually be losing money by doing it yourself.

I have found that having my son watch me do my work has saved me hundreds of hours as he teaches me computer shortcuts that reduce a great deal of time each month to a few clicks of the mouse! It can be worth it to hire even a high school student to help you automate tasks or learn how to use software to its fullest.

Once each task is either being done by someone else or is automated, you will be able to focus more on the three or four things in your circle. Your stress will go down and your income will go up!

It is easy to become distracted from the work that is billable and helpful to your clients. Always remember though that you need to focus on the things only you can do that will build your business.

Before you see the returning client

As a professional, you are expected to provide expertise for your clients. Taking a few minutes before the returning client enters your office will allow you to focus your thoughts and be prepared for the session.

Review your client file. This will help you to think about the topics from the previous sessions and the direction you will take for this appointment.

Gather any handouts or information that might be helpful for your client. Do you have an article, survey or book that might be a good to introduce? You might want to offer the business card or website of a resource. Having these things ready will save time and display your desire to assist the client.

Ensure that you are ready for the appointment. Make sure that you have eaten and been to the bathroom so that you can completely focus on the needs of the client. If your needs are met, the chances of meeting the needs of the client are reduced.

Survey the environment. Is it neat or are there things to be straightened or removed? Is the room temperature appropriate? What about noise? Adjusting the thermostat or playing soft music could greatly enhance the atmosphere and help your client to feel more comfortable.

Assemble the necessary items to facilitate the meeting. Do you have the file, paper for writing, pens or other tools ready? Make sure that there is bottled water available for you and the client.

Prepare items for discussion - Are there things that you need to review with the client before you begin the session? It is best to have all reports, documents or other items of concern ready so that they can be dealt with immediately and resolved at the beginning of the appointment.

Little things do make a difference. It is amazing how an investment of a few minutes can help both you and the client to have a more productive session together. It's all about being prepared.

Professional development

There is no maintenance in life. You are either moving forward or going backwards. Professional development is a way for you to move forward by increasing your knowledge, skills and abilities.

There are several things that you can include in your professional development plan including:

1. **Formal Training** - Universities and professional bodies often provide courses or programs where you can develop or enhance your knowledge and skills through scheduled classes.

2. **Internships** - You may be able to arrange a placement with another professional who can teach you about a specific topic and then supervise you as you develop expertise in that area.

3. **Conferences and Conventions** - Keynote speakers and break-out sessions often focus on new techniques or areas of practice.

4. **Developing a mastermind group** - Often individuals can learn from each other by forming a group with specific learning goals.

5. **Consultation** - Perhaps you can arrange to consult with an expert either in person or by telephone with a goal of mastering specific skills in an area of practice.

5. **Self-study** - Reading books or journals, researching on the Internet or interviewing individuals who are proficient in the topic area can all be ways to gain knowledge and expertise.

Technological advances have opened up almost unlimited opportunities for you to have interesting and creative professional development experiences. Webcams and teleseminars even allow you to learn from others in distant locations for a low cost without having to even leave home!

When it comes to professional development the only thing that might limit you is your imagination!

How to prevent formal complaints

It can be difficult, if not impossible, to keep everyone happy. Sometimes clients feel that they have not been treated properly and decide to file a formal complaint. There are several things that you can do to eliminate the risk of this happening as follows:

1. Only provide services in your area of competency. If you do not have expertise in the area that the client is seeking services, offer that person a good referral to another provider.

2. Be sure that the client has "Informed Consent". This means that the client knows exactly what you can and will do, your fees and how they are to be paid, limits to confidentiality, as well as an understanding of how you can help them.

3. Set clear goals with the client. You cannot "succeed" if you don't know exactly what needs to be accomplished. Often clients come to you without a clear picture of what needs to be resolved. Helping them to lay out the goals is an important part of the treatment plan.

4. Check with the client on a regular basis about the process. If you are truly interested in knowing how the person is doing and provide a safe environment where s/he can be honest, you will be able to make adjustments before there are major problems.

5. Listen in an open manner to concerns the client may have about you or the process. Clients can learn from your example and also will feel more comfortable knowing that your desire is to hear them and provide services that match their needs.

6. Consult with someone when you do not know how to resolve a situation. Often another perspective (and experience) will help you to consider options that would be helpful.

7. Deal with issues as they occur. Avoiding or procrastinating usually compounds what otherwise might be a simple problem.

8. If you don't hear from clients for a period of time, contact them to see if there are any things that you could do to help them.

9. Be honest. If you have made a mistake, admit it. Apologies are appropriate.

10. Offer to make appropriate referrals if the client no longer chooses to work with you.

Some clients may not be happy with your attempts to deal with issues but if you follow the above steps, you will likely be able to prevent formal complaints from being made against you.

Nobody likes to deal with clients who are unhappy but think of it this way: if we never hear about or face problems, we will never learn how to resolve them in a healthy manner. It is therefore important to hear the client's perspective and work to resolve the issues. That's what makes us better therapists in the long run.

What should you do if someone files a formal complaint against you?

Sometimes clients are unhappy with you and no matter what you do to resolve the situation, they decide to file a formal complaint against you. At other times, they might not even tell you before contacting your regulatory body.

There are several things that you should do if this happens:

1. **Don't panic** - This is not the end of the world and likely not the end of your career. The process for resolving the complaint may be long and stressful but it is important that you keep things in perspective. This is ONE complaint in the midst of many happy satisfied clients.

2. **Seek support** - Make sure you have opportunity to consult with someone in your profession who has experience and insight into the complaint process. Your family and friends may not understand the process whereas a peer will have understanding and can provide professional support for you.

3. **Don't expect things to be resolved immediately** - Bureaucracies are usually very slow and it may take months (or years) for an investigation to the completed.

4. **Contact Your Insurance Company** - As soon as you are aware that a formal complaint has been filed, contact the company that holds your liability insurance and provide them with all the details of the complaint.

5. **Obtain legal representation** - Your insurance company will likely recommend lawyers who have expertise in this field. It is acceptable to interview the lawyers they suggest until you find one who you want to have representing you.

6. **Review your file** - Go through the file to make sure that everything is in order. You cannot make changes to the notes and documents but you can ensure that everything is filed appropriately.

7. **Do not talk to the complainant or public about the complaint** -You will need to follow the advice of your lawyer. If you do need to talk, consider hiring a therapist to help you through the stress and respect your confidentiality.

8. **Continue to provide good service for your other clients -** You have an obligation to help your clients with their problems. Focus on them when you are with them.

9. **Take care of yourself** - Remember to use good health practices. Sleep, proper nutrition and exercise will help you to avoid illness and deal with this situation in the best way possible.

10. **Be honest** - If you did make a mistake, admit it. Perhaps you can take a weakness and turn it into strength with the appropriate help.

Formal complaints can place a great deal of pressure on you but you cannot focus all of your energy and attention on them. Remember to continue to enjoy your life, relationships and career.

Like my wise grandma used to say "This too shall pass".

Being an "expert" expert witness

Each of us is regularly asked to give opinions about our values, politics, community issues or other specific topics but most people go through life without having to formally witness in the justice system. Psychologists who work with individuals about legal matters, however, are often required to prepare reports or serve as witnesses in Court and this requires specific expertise.

A few years ago, I flew to Vancouver to attend a workshop entitled "Becoming an Expert Expert Witness" from Dr. Stanley L. Brodsky He is a professor at the University of Alabama whose work involves providing training and consultation for individuals who are required to give testimony in Court. He has written several books and developed considerable expertise in this niche.

For several hours we listened and learned from Dr. Brodsky so that we could develop skills for our careers. I realized, however, that the lessons he taught were valuable ones not only for Court purposes but also for daily living. In fact, many of them are ones that we teach children so that they will do well in society.

Whether you are in Court or in a social situation, you will do well to adopt Dr. Brodsky's advice:

1. Listen carefully and attentively to the question being asked. If you do not understand, ask for it to be repeated.

2. Be prepared. Knowing your subject means not only ongoing study but also being able to present information in a manner that can be understood.

3. Represent yourself well. Regardless of who pays you or influences you, what you say should be your opinion.

4. Be honest. It is okay to say "I don't know". Do not try to guess or make up an answer if you really don't know.

5. Relax. When you are feeling great pressure or stress, pause in order to allow yourself an opportunity to think before answering. Take a deep breath, release it and then answer.

6. Make eye contact with the person who is asking you a question.

7. Address the other person by his/her name.

8. Provide only the information that will answer the specific question and stop talking when you have done that.

9. Know your limits. You may be an expert in one area but no one is an expert at everything.

10. Admit any errors that you made have made and correct them immediately.

Whether you are speaking with a judge, your employer or your family members, the above guidelines will help you to develop a reputation of integrity and build trust with those who are interacting with you.

Planning Your Success

- ❑ Have you read your regulatory body's Standards of Practice?
- ❑ Do you have adequate insurance and required licenses?
- ❑ What will you do before seeing a new client?
- ❑ Do you know how to obtain Informed Consent?
- ❑ What are your limits to confidentiality?
- ❑ How will you ensure that documentation is done properly?
- ❑ How will you build and maintain a wonderful reputation?
- ❑ What will you do to meet your personal and professional needs?
- ❑ Do you know the five important things to do each day?
- ❑ How could you improve your focus?
- ❑ What will you do before you see a returning client?
- ❑ Do you have a written Professional Development plan?
- ❑ What things will you do to prevent formal complaints?
- ❑ What will you do if someone files a formal complaint?
- ❑ Are you prepared to serve as an Expert Witness in Court?

Notes:

Chapter Six

SECURING YOUR FINANCIAL HEALTH

A business plan is your career roadmap

A few years ago I decided to write a business plan for what was then a part-time endeavor. That year end I was shocked and pleased to discover that my income had increased by several thousand dollars over the previous year. This was a good return on my investment of only a few hours spent creating the plan.

Everyone knows that contractors do not begin working until they have a blueprint. Teachers develop a curriculum before starting a semester. Producers and directors require a script while sports enthusiasts play by rules and time limits that were previously established.

A story is told of the opening of *Epcot Center* in Florida. Walt Disney had died before the opening ceremony but his wife was in attendance for the ribbon cutting. A man leaned over to her and said "Too bad Walt wasn't here to see this". Mrs. Disney wisely replied "Oh, Walter saw this long before we did". You see, he had envisioned it and developed the plan so that it could be built.

**"We're devoting two years to develop a
five year plan to revise our three year plan
for the implementation of our ten year plan."**

Whether you are a large corporation, charitable organization or a small business, you need a business plan in order to have a clear vision of what you expect and how you will accomplish it in the next year. I challenge you to draw up the plan and then watch your goals and dreams come into reality.

If this is your first year of business, it is probably best to write a one-year plan and then use your year-end figures as a foundation for the next plan. Even though I have tried three-year plans, I really find the two-year ones the best length for me as they offer both short and longer-term goals.

The *Government of Canada* as well as many bank and business websites have software and examples that will assist you in developing your plan. You can access these without cost.

If you want to experience success, it is more important that you work ON your business than IN your business. This begins with writing your business plan! With a little effort and a lot of thought you will be able to experience the business growth that you personally designed.

Financial and banking options

Financial and banking systems are businesses that, like you, desire profit. They therefore charge you for each of the services that you choose - amounts which can drastically affect your bottom line. It is therefore important that you carefully analyze and make the best possible choices for your business. You will need to consider the following categories:

Personal accounts - Some people like to keep their personal and business accounts in separate banks thinking that by doing this they then have more privacy, control and benefits.

Others prefer the convenience of having all their accounts at the same place so that they can make one trip for transactions or easily transfer money between accounts. There may be discounts or financial advantages offered by the bank which result from having several services. These can appear in reduced interest rates, shares or preferred client services.

Business accounts - Because you are operating business - you need to have a business account that is separate from your personal funds. Be cautious when you choose the type.

- Will you pay a monthly fee or according to the number of transactions you make each month?
- Does your account have international options?
- Do you have free or reduced rates for safety deposit boxes or money orders?
- Can you use telephone or on-line banking without charge?
- Do you have a debit card or night depository option?
- What will cheques cost to order?
- Are there extra charges for you to receive your cancelled cheques?
- Would a Global Payment Card be offered to you (one in which you pay a merchant with the card but the funds come directly out of your account)?

- Can you set up a small overdraft protection to accommodate your contracted accounts receivables?

It is very important that you understand what is available and exactly what it will cost you. Make sure that you review your account each month so that you are aware of the charges you are paying.

Lines of credit - Starting, operating and expanding a business can place demands on your finances which may best be handled with a line of credit. Interest is only charged on the outstanding balance which can be paid throughout the month as funds are available. Although there isn't a minimum payment, most banks require that you pay down the interest that is accrued each month.

Loans - Start up can be costly and opening an office with furniture, equipment and the necessary business items might not happen unless you are able to secure an approved loan. You will need to provide the bank or credit union with documents that would convince them of your ability to repay the loan. Usually they require at least two years of Financial Statements but, if you are starting a new business they may require that you sign a personal guarantee and use your assets to secure the loan. The less risk the bank projects - the less the interest rate will be for you.

Credit cards – When it comes to choosing a credit card, the options are somewhat unlimited. Some business people choose their credit card according to the bank they use, the points they can accumulate or the interest rate that will be charged. Again you will need to be very cautious about your choice. Avoid those with annual fees and high interest rates. Ensure that you understand the repayment requirements - dates and amounts - so that you do not experience late-payment fees or an increase in the interest rate because you missed the payment cycle. A friend of my mother's used to say "If you can't make a payment this month, it sure won't be easier to make two next month". You goal for using credit cards is to pay the balance in full every month so that you will not build debt and have to pay interest.

Savings and investment accounts - You may choose to put your profits into bonds, short or long-term accounts, certificates or a number of other options. Research and discuss your options with a Financial Planner or accountant.

It is usually less expensive and more convenient to have only one chequing account (that pays interest on positive balances) and one credit card that is paid off each month. The rest can be unnecessary and expensive. Your business, however, is unique, and because of this, you will need to make unique and wise choices.

Accounts receivables

Accounts Receivables are monies that are owed to you for goods and services your clients didn't pay for when you provided them. When you allow a person to use your business as a "charge account", it costs you money. It is therefore important to always remember that this is your money so you need to have an excellent system for keeping track and collecting it.

When you see a client you should, if at all possible, collect the fee right after they receive the goods or service. I inform each person in advance that I only accept cash or cheque so that they are prepared when they come to the appointment. By doing this, you do not need to accept debit or credit cards and will save vendor fees that would otherwise be charged to you by merchant services.

At the first appointment, I also have the client sign an agreement which includes the fee, method and timing for payment. It also clearly defines if/how interest would be charged as well as my business policies and collections procedures for NSF cheques and unpaid accounts.

Immediately after the appointment prepare either a sales receipt (for cash or cheque) or an invoice (for third party payers). I never invoice companies or insurance plans on behalf of the client unless they have approved sessions in writing or signed a contract with me in advance.

My first choice for sending the invoices to the payee is by email or FAX as this saves time and the cost of postage.

At the end of each month prepare Account Statements for all clients who have unpaid balances. These need to be sent out immediately after the last day of the month.

I also like to print a listing of my Accounts Receivables for the month and then immediately make a plan to contact those which have been owed for the longest period of time. An email or polite telephone call can reveal the fact that the invoice had been misplaced, forgotten or missed the payee's payment cycle. Make sure that you ask when the account will be paid and document the answers you receive so that you can follow up if necessary.

Not collecting your Accounts Receivables on a regular basis is like losing your wallet. Somebody else has your money. What is the point of working hard if you are not going to be paid? Remember, this is a business and the money that is owed to you is your money.

If you have signed contracts with third party payees you will find that they usually have specific forms or requirements that must be met before they will make payment.

No matter what the client requires, you still need to have a business bookkeeping system that will record every single transaction in a standardized manner for your records. I use an amazing software program that allows me to set up each client and then do the invoicing and sales receipts with only a few clicks of the mouse! Simplicity is good and by being able to do my own entries while the client is present, I save the costs of hiring office staff.

If someone asked to borrow a large sum of money from you and repay it within 30 days, I think you would be watching the calendar and eager to collect, wouldn't you? Accounts receivables are the same thing. They allow the client to borrow your money while you wait for it. How much money are you prepared to lend to others?

The higher the balance on your Accounts receivable list, the more risk you place on your business. And the longer the balances are unpaid, the less chance you have of collecting them.

The buck stops with you! Go get your money - you earned it!

Taking financial retainers

There are times individuals pay or have a retainer paid on their behalf in advance of receiving services. This practice allows you to have more control, especially in cases where there is a risk that clients may decide not to pay you unless you say what they want you to say. It also allows you to have good cash flow while reducing your accounts receivable balance.

There are several things that you need to do before accepting any financial retainers:

1. **Ensure that taking retainers is allowed by your regulatory body** - Lawyers usually take retainers to cover hours of service that they will provide their clients in the future as well as costs for photocopying and filing Court documents. As the balance is used, they ask the client to "top up" the retainer balance. Not all professional bodies, however, allow you to take a retainer from your clients and you therefore need to make sure that you can legally and ethically do this before proceeding.
2. **Keep excellent records** - Make sure that you accurately document all the amounts received as well as the time and expenses which are applied to the retainer. I find that sending invoices to the clients as they occur helps them to understand how and when the money is being used.
3. **Know the rules and limitations regarding retainers** - Some laws require that you keep retainers in a separate bank account or have procedures that protect the money from being used inappropriately. Check with your regulatory body, lawyer and accountant regarding this.

4. **Give advance notice to clients or third-party payers regarding the need for additional funds**. I am working with a client whose fees are deducted from a retainer that is paid by her lawyer. After each appointment, I send the lawyer an invoice for the session as well as the balance of the account. I always advise the lawyer of the need to "top up" the account, allowing enough notice for the law office to prepare and mail a cheque to me before the retainer is depleted.

5. **Return any balances when the work is done** - It is very important that you return any balances to the client or payer after your services are complete. I suggest, however, that you have a discussion with the parties before cutting a cheque to ensure that your work really is done and then document that conversation. This prevents risk and embarrassment should you be asked to provide further services after the refund has been processed.

There are many times that I wished I had taken a retainer - especially in child custody and access cases. It is far easier to do this than to have to go to Small Claims Court in an attempt to collect unpaid fees. You will be able to focus better on the process and needs of the client when you are not concerned about payment for services. Taking a retainer for the work relieves you from the stress of wondering whether you will be paid.

Accounts payable

Accounts payables are the amounts that you owe vendors for goods or services that you received but haven't paid for yet. It is important to pay your accounts in a manner that will allow you to retain your reputation while maximizing your cash flow.

Following is the process that I find the most efficient for paying bills:

1. Record all regular payments with fixed amounts in your business calendar as recurring items so you will be reminded to pay them on time. These are payments for which you likely will not receive an invoice (for example, you rent payment).

2. Set up automatic recurring payments from your business account through your online banking. I prefer entering them myself rather than having the vendor set up automatic debits because I have more control. (This really helps if you are thinking about changing banks or vendors and want to ensure that automatic debits do not occur during the transition).

3. Enter the payment into your bookkeeping program as a debit for the date that the transaction will be processed.

4. Review all invoices on the day that they arrive for accuracy. Do not hesitate to delete interest that was incorrectly calculated and notify the vendor of any errors in the billing before you begin processing payment.

5. Enter the information from the invoice in the "Pay Bills" section of your bookkeeping software. Make sure that you date your payment so that it will be received no later than the due date but not too many days before the due date. That way you have use of the money in your account for as long as possible.

6. Use online banking to create a post-dated debit from your business account for the amount you will pay. (Banks recommend that you allow 3 to 10 days for processing so make sure that you date the debit accordingly). Print the online banking receipt and staple it to the invoice.

7. If the vendor requires a cheque and the invoice cannot be paid as an online debit, print the cheque and put it in an addressed envelope with a sticky note indicating the date that it is to be mailed in order to reach the vendor by the due date. Staple the cheque stub onto the front of the invoice.

8. File the paid invoices in folders that are properly labeled in a filing cabinet drawer with your other accounts payable documents.

It only takes a few minutes each month to process your accounts payables but doing so should be a priority. Handling them in an efficient and timely manner will save you time, late-payment charges, interest and build your reputation.

Remember, a good credit rating is, as the popular advertisement states "PRICELESS".

Payroll

Performing payroll activities can be a very difficult task. I remember working in a nursing home where there were about 50 staff, each with different rates of pay, hours and benefits. It was horrible!

I now have a beautiful and simple payroll program that practically runs itself!

You may not need a payroll system. In fact, if you are the only person who works in the business you may be taking dividends instead of a salary. Perhaps you are hiring people on a contract basis and do not offer payroll or benefit options. If this is the case, you merely cut a cheque for the amount that you have contracted.

For many years I was the only person in my business who had a full-time salary with benefits. I paid myself as though I was an employee so that I would have a regular income, accurate records and the ability to contribute to government pension programs. The only thing that I did not pay was Unemployment Insurance contributions because I would not be entitled to file a claim at any time due to the fact that I actually own the business. It felt good to get a regular cheque and the business classed my salary as an expense.

By setting up the payroll program to issue a cheque for me every second Friday, I received 26 cheques per year. In the early years or in times when I had extra expenses, I might print my cheque but not cash it for a couple of days. That way, the business had a little leeway but the paperwork was accurate.

Remittances for income tax and government pensions must be paid for all employees on either a monthly or quarterly schedule (as defined by the government). Penalties can be levied for late payment so I was always extremely careful to pay all remittances on time.

If you are paying yourself a salary, your accountant will work with you to determine if adjustments should be made to your payroll source deductions. You can increase them to avoid having to pay additional taxes at year end or decrease them to allow for any RRSP contributions or additional deductions you may have.

Government policies and procedures usually change each year as do income tax laws. It is therefore important that you have a good accountant and payroll software program that will update you and help to make the necessary adjustments as they occur. Rather than buying a packaged payroll program, consider an online monthly program as you will then receive all updates automatically and not have to keep replacing the whole program when changes occur.

This year my accountant, financial planner and I decided that it was financially wiser for me to not be classed as a salaried employee. Instead, I write myself dividend cheques on dates of my choosing and invest business profits in accounts that are set up within the business. This system makes a significant financial difference for me and for the business.

It is important that you consult with experts before you decide how you will pay yourself for your work. Make sure that you fully understand all the tax implications, as well as the advantages and disadvantages before you make a final decision regarding this.

Make good hiring choices

When you work hard, you expect to enjoy the profits of your business. One of the largest expenses you will ever face will likely be for staffing. Your business profits can quickly disappear into salaries and benefits if you aren't careful.

Salaried employees: Having salaried employees is a very expensive proposition and I really discourage it. A full-time staff member gets paid even if you are away from the office. Besides their hourly or yearly salary, you are also required to pay employer contributions for them which usually adds at least 17% more to your expenses. Their holidays and sick leave days are also paid even though you do not have productivity during those hours.

The advantage of having salaried employees, of course, is that you are guaranteed that they will be available for you during the hours you have specified for the job. Loyalty also can also be established when your staff members believe that they have security in their employment but you need to seriously weigh the facts and decide whether these benefits are worth the costs.

Hourly employees: When you do not require full-time help, you might consider hiring individuals who can work for you during part-time scheduled hours, flexible hours or on a casual basis. The advantage of hiring part-time or casual employees, of course is that your costs can be controlled. You likely will not offer or pay benefits for them and can choose the number of hours that you can afford.

The disadvantage of hiring on a part-time basis is that some people require full-time wages and you therefore might be only one of their employers. If this is the case, your needs may not get priority.

Contracted help: You might prefer to contract with a person or organization to complete projects for you rather than hire staff. For example, setting up a computer system, creating a marketing plan or performing accounting services might be best done by contract.

Ensure that you are clear about what you need, obtain quotes and set a date for evaluation before you sign your contract so that you can ensure that you will get what you need and want for the best possible price. Make sure you negotiate when and how the contract will be paid. (And remember to negotiate. Just because someone gives you a quote doesn't mean that you have to accept it!).

Family members as staff: One of the benefits of owning your own business is that you can hire family members to perform business tasks. The double benefit is that they have some income and you have a write-off for income tax purposes. Win/Win!

Before you can hire anyone to work for you, you must be very clear about what you need and what you expect. Otherwise, you will likely be trusting someone to read your mind - and that can be costly!

It is always a good idea to write a list of tasks that need to be done and the expected time it will take to complete them. Be clear with the person you hire regarding what you want them to do through a written job description and a verbal discussion before they begin working for you.

10 ways you can save money or increase profit

As a solo professional, you are dealing with investing your own time, energy and money on a daily basis. Your profit is based on the number of billable hours you complete less your expenses.

Following are ten specific things that will make your practice more profitable:

1. **Research** - There is so much competition in the marketplace that investing a little bit of time to research your options to lower expenses can often save a great deal of money for you. Telephone plans, office equipment or insurance rates are good examples of costs which can greatly vary in price. Sometimes an Internet search or a telephone call will help you to find a "better deal". You need to be careful however, that the goods or services are the same and that you do not risk losing benefits in the name of price.

2. **Negotiate** - My son-in-law is a salesman who negotiates EVERYTHING. Sometimes my daughter is embarrassed when he asks for a discount on items but he usually gets one. Most companies and employees have the ability to reduce prices. All you need to do is ask.

3. **Understand the difference between needs and wants** - Before you buy anything ask yourself "Do I really NEED this?" The answer will involve a process of determining the number of times you will use the item and whether another less expensive one will

do just as well. This is about getting your business and personal needs met and not about filling your ego.

4. **Take advantage of timing** - Most items are cheaper at certain times of the month or year. Buying a car, for example, can be less expensive at the end of the month (if the salesman wants to meet a quota) or in the fall (when the new models arrive). You might want to purchase office supplies in August when the back-to-school sales are on. Remember to ask your accountant to help you schedule purchases for larger items so you will have the best tax advantage.

5. **Buy in quantity**- Sometimes you can save a great deal of money by making bulk purchases. For example, buying two cases of paper instead of one might offer a good saving or placing an order of a specified amount might result in you not having to pay shipping charges. Even signing specific contracts, such as your office lease, for longer periods of time might provide discounts for you. The key, of course, is that you really need the products or services and are only investing your money where you will gain clear benefits.

6. **Avoid interest costs** - Interest is toxic in that it eats away at your profit. It is therefore very important that you pay all of your bills on time each month. Companies charge as much as 30% interest for late or unpaid bills and it doesn't take long until the amount you initially owed them is doubled. On the other hand, you can actually save thousands of dollars a year by paying your credit card balances in full each month or by having a lower-rate line of credit instead of a credit card.

7. **Know the consequences of penalties and bank charges** - Banks tend to charge a number of fees to maintain accounts and if you are not aware of these, you can pay a significant amount that is not necessary. Check your bank statements and question anything that is listed. There might be a different plan that would better suit your needs for a lower cost. Also, be aware of and avoid incurring penalties and late payment charges. You might be charged as much as $50.00 for an NSF cheque or as an addition to interest for late payment on a credit card (and lose your reputation and lower interest rate). Sometimes fees can be

more than the payment that is due or even the balance that is owed! Be careful!

8. **Consider ways you can earn additional income** - Are you using your office all the time or could you possibly rent it out to another professional? Over the years I have paid at least half of my lease each month by sub-letting the office on specific days of the month. An added benefit is that having someone else use your office space keeps you out of it! You are not tempted to work too hard when you have someone else using the space. There are many other ways to increase your income and profit such as writing a book, contracting paid speaking engagements or charging clients for handouts and/or photocopying.

9. **Keep it simple** - The more paperwork you do the more expensive it is – for paper and ink, storage and accounting fees. You also need to remember that the professionals who help with your business charge by the hour so the more often you meet with or contact them, the more you will pay in fees. Ask your accountant, lawyer or other professionals what they need from you and provide it without discussing all the details or engaging in "chit chat". Remember, the clock is running and you are paying!

10. **Hire family** - I have two of three children and four of six grandchildren who work with me. They are always so creative in showing me how their skills and abilities can be used to prosper my business. When you hire family, you provide them with income, watch them develop loyalty and understanding about your career and have an opportunity to teach them about professionalism. You might also, within limits, be able to use their work hours as a business tax deduction. Your accountant will be able to advise you regarding this.

President Harry S. Truman had a sign on his White House desk that stated "The buck stops here". As a solo professional, you have the responsibility to make decisions that will help to reduce expenses and increase profit.

Be wise for the buck stops with you!

Building your professional team

Over the years, I have developed an amazing team of professionals who have provided me with information and support.

You and your business will benefit from building relationships with individuals in the following roles:

1. **Lawyer** - I actually have more than one lawyer. Because my office is in the same building as a law firm, I have the advantage of being able to talk with any of their staff about my office lease or changes within the legal system. I also have a lawyer who is an expert on liability who I can consult for professional client issues and a personal lawyer who has helped me to write my will.

2. **Accountant** - I tried working with a large national firm but did not like receiving huge bills for services that I wasn't sure were needed. Now I contract with a woman who has a private business and pay her by the hour. She is a wonderful advocate, knows the income tax laws extremely well and doesn't hesitate to contact Revenue Canada if she has a question. She completes and submits all the forms that are required by the government - payroll remittances, Good and Services Tax (GST), annual income tax returns and financial statements.

3. **Banker** - I find it better to deal with the Manager of my Credit Union than with a Customer Service Representative because I know she will be there when I need her. This is not always the case with bank staff who change jobs frequently. The Manager has the ability to get my requests met in good time because she supervises all staff and departments. She and I usually communicate through email and this saves a great deal of time in comparison to having to book appointments.

Besides the named professionals I also value my insurance broker, travel agent, doctor, virtual assistant, "techie", hairdresser and all those who help me to be my best so that I can offer my best to others!

Build your professional team and value them. They help you and your business to look good, be healthy and act professionally.

Goal setting and reviewing your progress

It would be very difficult to leave your home and try to locate a destination where you have never visited - especially if you don't have a map! Many business professionals do not know where they want to go or how to get there. It is important that you set up road markers and watch for them as you travel each business day.

1. **Your business finances** - Do you know your bank balance? What would it be if all your cheques cleared or if all your bills were paid? Do you have a credit card balance? What is the interest rate and amount you paid in fees and interest this year? If you do not know these figures, you are flying blind. Hope will not get you where you want to be. Pull out your bank and credit card statements for the past six months. Take time to read everything on each page and add up the charges you have incurred. You might be shocked by the situation.

2. **Your sales goal -** Do you know the amount of sales that you need each month to pay all your expenses? How many billable hours do you need each week? Do you check your progress on a daily basis? As a solo professional, you are the only employee. Are you a good employee? Perhaps you are not working enough hours or not billing for all the services you are providing. Maybe you need to do more marketing. If you are not meeting your sales goals and not doing anything to improve that, it is only a matter of time until you will have to close the doors of the business.

3. **Your expenses** - Do you know how much it costs every month to operate your business? Are there months when these are significantly higher? Do you have a plan to pay bills as close to the due date as possible to avoid interest? Are there things that you are buying that you could do without? How can you reduce your expenses?

4. **Your credit information** – Your financial reputation is based on data collected by different agencies such as Equifax and Transunion. When you apply for a credit card or loan, this information is requested from the credit agency and approval is based on whether you are classed as a good risk. Unfortunately sometimes what is on file is not accurate. It is your responsibility to review your credit report and ensure that the corrections are made.

    Your credit score is a number that rises and falls according to the amount of credit you have at the time, your payment history and the amount of activity on your file. The higher the score, the better you are viewed when it comes to granting further credit.

    It is very important that you request copies of your credit report on a regular basis. You can request a free copy by mail or for a small fee can get instant access over the Internet. I request and review my credit report twice a year so that I am aware of what is on my file and can ensure it is accurate.

5. **Your marketing plan** - How will you attract clients to your business? Do you have effective, low-cost strategies to advertise or promote your services? How many new clients have you seen this year? How did they hear about you? What things have you been planning to do to increase your referral sources that you just haven't done yet?

6. **Your future** - Do you have a plan for retirement? Is your business saleable? Does your will clearly state your wishes regarding the business? Do you have family members who can take over at some point?

Showing up at the office is not enough! You need to decide where you want to go with the business and then have a road map that will ensure you arrive safely and on time!

Three mistakes that solo professionals make

Sometimes professionals have expertise in their chosen field but do not do well in their practice. They want to have their own business but cannot seem to earn enough money to do so.

There are three mistakes that solo professionals make which stop them from having success in business:

1. **Lack of focus** - When Tiger Woods was asked why he was such a good golfer, he came up with an excellent answer. He said "I focus better than other people". He has wind, television cameras and spectators as distractions. If he doesn't focus on the ball he will not hit it.

    Solo professionals do not always focus on the activities that are billable - seeing clients and doing things that can be invoiced. Sitting on committees, doing community service and attending workshops may be interesting but they should be planned so that they are not done instead of the things that lead to profit.

    Examine your day. Do you focus on the things that bring sales and income into your business? If not, it's time to make adjustments.

2. **Over-spending** - Do you really need that expensive vehicle or computer system? Are you trying to maintain a status that is beyond your financial means? Many professionals spend money they don't have with the idea that they will earn it in the future. In the meantime they pay for it over and over again in interest costs.

    Consider what you really NEED to operate your business.

    I have met with clients in offices that I rented by the hour, provided telephone therapy and made do with an office where we shared a bathroom with others in the building - just to keep costs down. It is far better to earn money that isn't committed than to face the stress of thinking that you have to "perform" in order to survive financially.

3.   **Trying to do everything** - When you think that you must perform
     all the tasks of a busy office, you jeopardize your health, energy
     level and future. Many professionals come to me with a diagnosis
     of depression but, when I complete an assessment, I realize that
     they are really in a state of being "overwhelmed".

Take time to examine the things you are doing and decide if some of
them can be done by others. Often you can work one additional hour
a day to earn the amount you would need to hire someone for 8 or 10
hours to do specific tasks that you might otherwise be doing.

Ensure that you have people in your life who will be honest with you
about your self-care. It is easy to forget to eat or not get enough sleep
but a caring friend or family member will help you to get back on track.
Working smart is better than working hard.

As a solo professional, you will need to protect yourself - professionally,
financially, physically and mentally - so that you can carry on in your
business without interruption.

Life is a series of choices - make good ones!

Planning Your Success

- ☐ Do you have a written Business Plan?

- ☐ Have you considered your financial and banking options?

- ☐ Do you understand the importance of Accounts Receivables?

- ☐ How will you handle financial retainers for future services?

- ☐ Do you have a system for Accounts Payable?

- ☐ Do you need to have a payroll system?

- ☐ What is your hiring process?

- ☐ Are you confident that you can make good hiring choices?

- ☐ Do you know ways to save money and increase your profit?

- ☐ How will you build your professional team?

- ☐ Did you write out your goals?

- ☐ When and how will you review your progress?

- ☐ How will you avoid the 3 mistakes solo professionals make?

Notes:

Chapter Seven

SATISFYING YOUR PERSONAL AND PROFESSIONAL NEEDS

Be well-seasoned in your life

I've loved food my whole life. I love buying groceries, looking at weekly flyers and taste testing new recipes. I love restaurants and invitations to friends' for dinner and eating at home. I love lunch and dinner but mostly I love snacks. Ice cream cones, cookies, cheese cake, pies, rice pudding, chocolate covered almonds, muffins, O Henry bars... Yes, I love food ... and the Food Channel. The trouble is that every show seems to feature a chef who loads their recipes with everything that my doctors (and common sense) warn me against - like sugar, butter, salt and various types of cream.

One of the things that I have learned about cooking from the Food Channel though is the importance of seasonings. Frequently the host of the program uses home-grown vegetables, spices and herbs to give flavour to their cuisine. Garlic, onions, rosemary, thyme, lemon, or cilantro are added to the bland in order to bring life and interest for the diner.

The term "season" has a number of meanings. We offer "season's greetings" at Christmas, think of the changing seasons and even describe someone who is experienced as being "well-seasoned".

One year, my friend, Carla, sent me an electronic birthday card that featured jazzy music, flashing graphics and a food theme. It suggested that we should "be well seasoned", "peppery", "salt of the earth" and not bland or lumpy. It even went so far as to recommend that we "Don't turn into comfort food - easily managed and twice as tasteless".

Sometimes people in our lives or our experiences change our true essence through criticism or unrealistic demands. Frequently my clients tell me that they just don't know themselves anymore or are tired of trying to live up to everyone's expectations. They have lost their seasoning and don't seem to think they can recover until they leave home, finalize a divorce, or move to a different job or city.

Seasoning has to be done in a way that enhances the result but taste is based on individual preference. You cannot season to please others only to find that life gives you a bad taste in your mouth. Being well seasoned every season of your life requires understanding of yourself, what season of life you are in and the options that you have to spice it up.

It is important that you examine both your life and your business in order to determine exactly what you want from each. As a solo professional, you have the opportunity to plan the menu and then create a unique flavour that you will enjoy. It's all up to you!

Bon apetit!

Keep it simple!

Life is complex and at times it can become confusing when it comes to deciding what you have to do. In fact, when you are opening or operating a business it is easy to become overwhelmed and get off track.

If you focus on the following five things you will be able to do well in your business and your personal life:

1. **Provide billable services** - If you aren't making money, you aren't in business. There are specific activities which you must do in order to earn money. Be very clear about what these are and invest most of your day doing them. If you find yourself doing things that cannot be invoiced, you need to re-adjust.

2. **Observe honest, ethical practices** - Make sure that what you do in both your personal and business life is honest and ethical. As a solo professional, there is a very thin line between the two and what you do affects everything else. Many people have large incomes that they gain through illegal or immoral activities. Your reputation is based on your practices and you will not have an opportunity to enjoy the fruits of your labour if you are in jail!

3. **Do your paperwork** - Many professionals procrastinate in doing their paperwork and then try to justify this by stating that they focus on clients instead. Both are necessary but if you have not updated your files, done your bookkeeping or filed documents within the expected time lines, you will jeopardize your business and waste time. I once returned from my holidays to find out that a baby on my caseload had died. The file was given to the investigators and I didn't have access to it again. How thankful I was that all my notes and documents had been completed before I had left for my holidays. You never know when you will be held accountable for your work and therefore need to have everything done up to date. Courts generally observe the unwritten rule that notes made within 48 hours of an incident are best.

4. **Pay your bills on time** - It may seem like common sense to do this but I have been surprised over the years to learn how many people who describe themselves as professional do not have a good financial reputation. I'm sure that you want to be paid on time for your work and others feel the same way. When you owe money to your vendors you risk tarnishing your reputation. If you cannot afford to pay the balance in full, at least call the vendor, send post-dated cheques or make regular payments until the balance is paid

in full. (And do not expect the vendor to do you any favours or provide further services in the meantime).

5. **Practice self-care** - You are the business and it is therefore important that you protect your physical and mental health. That way you will be able to continue to work and enjoy the benefits earned in the business for years to come.

There are many distractions that interfere with people's ability to do well. Ensure that you are doing all of the above and you will soon develop good habits that will build your business in a healthy manner.

Be well in order to do well

Your physical and mental health are both vital to your business. You see, as a solo professional you are the only one who can do the work and generate an income. Poor health will jeopardize everything.

But, it works both ways. Business can also jeopardize your health if you aren't careful. I have worked with many individuals over the years who do not protect themselves and end up losing both their health and their careers.

There are several things that you need to do on a regular basis in order to maintain the health that will allow you to build your business and enjoy your life:

Sleep – I often tell my clients that I am like a baby. If I don't eat right and don't sleep – I cry. Most people do not have an established routine that will allow them to get at least eight hours of uninterrupted sleep each night. And then they wonder why they are not feeling or doing well.

Bedrooms should be used only for sex and sleep. Ensure that you have a dark and quiet room with comfortable bed and bedding. Remove televisions, computers and other activities that might distract you from falling or staying asleep. This is not the time to plan tomorrow's agenda or balance your chequebook in your head. When you lie down, use self-talk that will relax you.

One of the very best things that you can do for yourself is to ensure that you are well rested before you begin each day. When you do, everything will seem just a little bit better!

Diet - Food is the fuel that fires your brain and body. Just as you wouldn't put sugar in the gas tank of your vehicle and expect it to operate well you shouldn't expect your body to work well if all you give it is an unhealthy diet.

Balance your day with small meals that consist of fruit, vegetables, dairy, breads and protein. Make water your first beverage choice. Limit your intake of caffeine, alcohol and sugar. Try packing lunches and snacks so you aren't tempted to make poor choices by slipping out of the office for junk food.

Examining your diet will help you to understand why there have been times that you felt you didn't reach your potential.

It is true that "you are what you eat" and you therefore need to make good food and beverages choices.

Exercise – Are you physically active? How often and how much do you move? Are you a regular gym enthusiast, long-distance runner or member of a sports team? Keeping active will not only help your body to function well but also improve your mood as your endorphins are activated.

But you don't have to be an Olympic athlete to build good physical health. In fact, you can change your sedentary lifestyle to one of active living by making small choices in the day. Try taking the stairs instead of the elevator. Park a little further from your destination in order to add a few more steps to your day. Even working in an office all day in a stationary position can be broken up with simple exercises or activity during lunch and other breaks.

If you choose to participate in things that you enjoy doing, you will likely be more disciplined. Think about the things that you did frequently as a child and you will soon have good ideas about how to develop a fitness plan. When I was younger I enjoyed swimming but because of my busy schedule, it was hard to get to a community pool. I decided that it was important for me to become more active and therefore sold my townhouse and moved into a condo that has a swimming pool. Now I can get my exercise at all hours of the day or evening without having to leave home.

Make a plan that will work for you!

Have regular checkups - Visit your doctor and dentist at least yearly. These professionals will identify any possible health problems in the early stages so that treatment can be started and help you to make good choices to maintain your well-being.

Protect your mental health - Learn how to reduce and deal with stress. Develop your communication skills. Ensure that you have good boundaries. Schedule activities that are fun and relaxing for you.

My grandpa used to say "If you have your health you can make your wealth". That is true. Your health affects your business but your business also affects your health. The choices you make in each will either help or harm the other. Ensure that your choices are good ones.

And remember, you are the business so taking care of your health means that your business will be less vulnerable.

Balance work and home

In "The Places You'll Go" Dr. Seuss wrote "Life is one great balancing act".

Everyone has demands at work and at home so it is important that each of us learns how to cope with all of them and find a healthy balance.

I remember a few years ago when a secretary came into my office and plunked herself down on a chair. She said "I know you have problems but every day you come into the office and with a big smile say 'Good morning'. No one would ever know there was anything wrong in your life. How do you do it?"

My answer was simple. I said "I learned a long time ago that when I am at work I focus on work and when I am at home I focus on my personal life." That takes discipline but it really helps to reduce stress and increase productivity.

Every day I use this strategy. My clients know that when I am with them - I am totally with them. Nothing breaks my concentration or interrupts me. My children, grandchildren and friends experience the same thing. I totally focus on them when we are together.

During an interview a few years ago, Tiger Woods was asked how he has become such an outstanding golfer. I thought that he gave the most interesting response. He said "I know how to focus better than anyone else". You see, on the golf course he is faced with so many distractions such as wind, television cameras and fans. If he doesn't focus on the ball, he won't hit it.

As a child, Tiger's father wanted him to learn how to focus so, in an effort to train him, Mr. Woods would walk behind Tiger and drop a number of golf clubs just as Tiger was ready to swing. Over time, Tiger learned to focus on the ball despite what could be distractions that were near him. I am sure that he does not take this strength for granted and likely tries every day to improve his focus.

When your attention is divided, you do not do as well as when you are focused. In fact, problems and issues are more easily and quickly resolved when you devote all your time and attention to them. It is therefore better to divide things into categories and deal with them one at a time.

There are three things that you can do that will allow you to be less stressed and more productive:

1. Each night, before you leave the office develop a list of things that you need to do the following day. A list saves you from having to remember everything and gives you a boost when you can check things off as they are completed.
2. Set up healthy boundaries to protect the time which might otherwise be robbed by co-workers who want to "chat" or family members who frequently call you at work.
3. Train your mind to stay in the moment and focus on what is before you.

Balancing your work and home life can be a daunting task, but with commitment and practice you will soon learn the skills that will have you managing things like a pro!

Know what you want

As a solo professional, you have the ability to tailor your business to meet your wants as well as your needs. I have found that there is great freedom in knowing that I can choose the type of clients, hours of work and areas of focus that will bring satisfaction to my day.

A couple of years ago, I realized that there are some things that only I can do because of my knowledge, skills, abilities, and credentials. For example:

THERAPY - I am a Registered Psychologist and Registered Social Worker who has certificates in several specialties. I cannot hire someone to do the assessments or treatment that my clients need.

SPEAKING - When I am contracted to do a presentation or workshop, I am the one who is responsible to do this. The organization expects me to be there and offer my best to the audience.

WRITING - Although some people have a ghost writer, I feel that it is important for me to do all the writing for articles and newspaper columns myself.

Sometimes I hire or contract others to do activities that are not in those areas or to support me in those roles. If I find myself constantly working on projects outside of these three roles, however, I need to be thoughtful about this and adjust accordingly.

What are the things that you want to do? Do you want to write a book, offer speeches for cruise lines or limit your work week to three days? What you want to do and what you need to do can be very different but, when you have your own business you do have the opportunity to create a world where both needs and wants can be satisfied. The key is in the planning!

Begin by sitting down right now and, on a blank piece of paper, describe your "dream job". What skills do you have that you could provide through service to others for a fee? What might you need to learn or develop before that could happen? Where would you like to work? Would you like to be a solo professional or begin by working with others?

Everything begins with an idea. When you have a very clear idea about the business you would like to have, it will be easier to turn that into reality.

Enjoy your work

Often it is the little things that help you to enjoy your life and work.

Think about what you can do to change or improve things so you will really look forward to going to the office every day. You might begin by:

1. **Scheduling interesting work hours** - I am NOT a morning person and many of my clients need evening appointments

so I adjust my office hours to accommodate this. Consider the times of the day when you are at your best and build your business based on this.

2. **Implementing rest periods and breaks** - I do better when I have at least 15 minute breaks between clients. This gives me time to complete the file notes, visit the bathroom and rest my eyes. I also have an alarm clock which has allowed me at times, to have a short nap on one of my love seats during an open appointment time.

3. **Setting up a pleasant environment** - If I am going to spend several hours at the office, I know that I will be comfortable because I have decorated it to my personal tastes. I also have a fridge, microwave and table so I can enjoy lunch or snacks while I am there.

4. **Establishing healthy boundaries** - I no longer take cases that are stressful for me. There are certain areas of work that I find more enjoyable so I tend to take referrals for those instead. It is better to focus on work that I enjoy rather than being worn down by stressful cases. I also choose co-workers, clients and my friends with care as I want to be around people who are positive rather than those who have toxic attitudes.

5. **Embracing variety** - I like providing therapy for clients but also enjoy writing, teaching and speaking engagements. Because of this I have designed my business to include all of these activities.

6. **Learning to handle cycles** – There are times when you will be extremely busy and times when you will wonder if the bottom is falling out. Every business has cycles. It is important that you work hard during the busy times and learn to relax during the quieter times. Catch up on your reading, create new handouts, or work on your marketing and networking goals when you are not seeing clients. You will feel less stress during the slower seasons if you have set up your finances so it won't feel like "feast or famine".

If you are not enjoying your work or some aspects of it, you need to be honest with yourself about this. Write down all the things that drain you and then decide how you might be able to implement changes that will bring more satisfaction for you. Perhaps you can hire someone to do certain tasks, automate them or eliminate them altogether.

Remember, this is your business and you therefore get to design your own job description and career path.

Earn an appropriate income

"Of course money can buy happiness!
Why do you think I charge $250 an hour?"

There are advantages and disadvantages to owning a business. Even though you are the boss and can therefore take time off whenever you choose to do so, you will still need to work enough to make a good profit and set up a plan that will provide you with ongoing income when you are away from the office or quit working altogether.

Everyone deserves to have a good return on investment but, there are times when you, as a solo professional, will likely earn less than you might as an employee or in very prosperous economic times.

A person can only invest their time and energy for a certain period of time without receiving an income that will meet their personal and family needs. The key is therefore to have a business plan that includes marketing to attract new clients, a competitive but fair fee schedule and a commitment to work enough hours that will generate desired profit.

You must have a clear plan for how you will be reimbursed for your work or you will quickly lose your enthusiasm for the business as well as your financial well-being.

Consider talking with others about the many options that you have available to you:

Employee - I have an incorporated company and, when I first starting in private practice, set myself up as an employee who received a pay cheque every second Friday. Mind you, when I was building the business, I certainly did not have as large a cheque as I had been earning as a public sector employee. There were even times when I wouldn't cash my cheque for a few days because there wasn't enough money in the account. I chose to be an employee though because I liked the idea of having a regular pay day and the ability to pay into a company-matched pension and benefit plan.

Owner – Recently my accountant, financial planner and I worked together to restructure the way I receive income from the business. Instead of being an employee, I now take "draws" or "dividends" from the business account when I want them for personal reasons. The amounts usually vary based on what I need, why I am taking them, and, of course, how much money is available in the business account at the time.

We have also set up an investment plan where I can watch pre-tax dollars grow within the business. This fund replaces contributions that I had previously been making to the Canada Pension Plan which the business was required to match on my behalf. There are a significant financial and tax advantages to doing this.

I lease my personal vehicle to the business for a monthly fee for example and have a company-paid employee benefit plan that covers my medical and dental expenses. I also enjoy opportunities when I can add a couple of extra days to business trips where the major expenses for hotel and flights are paid for by my corporation.

You see, there are tax and personal advantages to being an owner rather than an employee. Talk with your accountant and financial planner to make sure that you understand the best way to maximize profit while, at the same time, adhering to good accounting practices and government requirements.

You also, of course, have to make sure that you are working enough billable hours and generating enough profit to fund everything that you want from the business.

Commissioned Worker - Perhaps you will establish a commission schedule and pay yourself a percentage of the amount you invoice. This system will provide you with an incentive if you are the kind of person who is motivated by plans in which the more you do, the more you earn.

You might even set up a commission scale to pay yourself at different rates for specific things. For example, if you have published a book, your income on sales might be percentage that is different from the one you take on therapy fees.

Retiree/Former Owner - Having a plan to sell your business or transfer it into the hands of family members in the future can be created with the help of other professions. You might decide to have a business appraisal done and then sell the business for a specific amount. A lawyer and/or accountant can also help you to consider how you might be able to show you ways that you can receive ongoing income through dividends or shares based on future profits or consulting fees.

If you have established a division of your business that sells books or other copywrited materials you might choose to not include this in the sale or transfer of the business so you will have ongoing income.

Travel for business and pleasure

Many professionals enjoy travelling but feel that they cannot take a holiday because there is no one to take care of business while they are away. This is a dangerous fallacy that can rob you of your health and well-being.

Everyone deserves time off and, in fact, most of us are better able to serve others after we have had a break. Being away from the office on a regular basis is something that is done by most healthy individuals.

You are not invincible! You need to look after yourself and one of the greatest self-care strategies is to plan time away from the demands of your work.

In order to do this, you will need to do some planning so that your needs and the needs of your clients are met:

1. **Schedule time off well in advance and mark the time you will be away on your calendar** - This time is sacred and should NOT be changed for any reason (except serious illness or death of you or a family member).

   I respect my clients by scheduling time for them and I respect myself by scheduling time for me. If a client asks to book an appointment when I will be away I don't get into explanations but merely state "I'm already booked".

   By the way, it is easier to avoid the temptation to cancel any time off if you already have tickets or committed plans to be out of town.

2. **Inform your clients of their options during the time you will be away** - Most people will not be in crisis or need to access other services while you are gone. They are used to booking appointments with professionals based on what is available for them. It is a good idea, however, for them to know that they can go to the emergency department at the hospital if they need priority services.

194

If someone is answering your calls while you are away there is really no reason to even tell the clients that you are not available.

Usually the client is happy to have your scheduler book an appointment time for them and do not expect more than that.

A couple of times when I was out of country I did return calls from clients who stated they were in a crisis. In a matter of a few minutes we were able to de-escalate the situation.

Most clients tend to calm down significantly once they hear your voice and a brief conversation provides an opportunity for you to do some planning and crisis management.

You might also want to arrange with another therapist to handle any crisis situations that might come up when you are away but will likely find that this backup situation will be more for your peace of mind than anything else.

3. **Limit your time away -** I tend to book time off in small increments that are no longer than seven days in duration. Also, I often go away in the middle of a week and return in the middle of the next week. Doing this means that it doesn't seem to be so long for clients as it is just two or three days out of two weeks rather than a full week.

4. **Ensure that your clients have appointments booked before you leave** - They will feel more content, knowing that they have a time set up and this will reduce the number of voice mail messages you will deal with when you return.

5. **Change your voice mail message and/or check it each day that you are away** - If you or your scheduling staff return calls during your time off, many people will not even know you are away. Make sure your voice mail message clearly states the date that you will be returning calls and asks the clients to specify the purpose of their call. This will help you to triage for crisis and deal with only top priority issues during your time away.

6. **Combine business and pleasure** - Add a couple of days to a workshop or convention so that you can enjoy the city where

this is being held. Search for opportunities to meet individuals or visit organizations in the area that have inspired you or might have lessons for you to learn. When you combine business and pleasure, you can also take advantage of tax deductions for the business activities.

7. **Bring back items or stories that will enhance your practice and inspire your clients** - Many of my trips have provided wonderful experiences which I have been able to use to help clients. My first book, for example, is about ten life lessons that I learned while travelling in different cities. Travel with a mindset that is open to new ideas and both you and your clients will be richly rewarded!

It is possible (and necessary) to "get away from it all" once in awhile but doing so will require planning so that your needs and the needs of your clients will be met while you are away.

Don't procrastinate. Begin now. Take out your calendar and begin planning an adventure!

Working with family members

One of my dreams has always been to build a business in which all of my family members have an opportunity to use their skills and gifts if they choose to do so.

At this time I have two of three children and four of six grandchildren on staff. My daughter is my business assistant who handles contract negotiation and client scheduling virtually as she lives three hours from my office. My older son does all my technological work, graphic design and accompanies me for professional speaking engagements. He lives five hours from my office. One grandchild works on social media. Another produces products that are for sale. A third grandson serves as my janitor. My granddaughter is the office librarian.

None of my family lives in the city where I live but many of the tasks that they do are over the Internet or can be accomplished when they visit me.

There are both advantages and disadvantages to having family members work with you in your business.

One strong advantage is that there is far less training than if you hired a stranger. Family members know you and your style as well as the values that you wish to honour.

The grandchildren are usually thrilled to have the opportunity to earn a cheque which they might not otherwise have had. You also have the precious thrill of working with and teaching them skills that will last a lifetime. And, as long as the family members are doing work that will build or maintain your practice their wages are a business expense.

Working with family can also cause problems, especially if boundaries aren't strong. Because you have known each other for years and years, there is a "history" which can interfere with the working relationships and emotions can, at times, run high. As much as you may want to, you cannot easily fire someone to whom you gave birth!

If you are planning to work with family members it is important that you have clearly defined roles for each of you. You must be prepared for differences of opinion that might be rooted in past issues. Being able to work through problems will likely be beneficial for everyone - if the process is a healthy one.

The most important thing to remember is that this is your business and you are the boss. Because of that, you have the responsibility to make the final decision on everything. You cannot micro-manage your family members but you need to ensure that you and your family members know that you are the Chief Executive Officer.

Re-assessing to improve the business

Once your business is established you might find that it isn't working exactly the way that you had dreamed it would or just want to make a few changes to improve things.

Would you like to expand your business? Are there things that need to be changed? Do you have some secret dreams that you hope you will "someday" achieve? What are you waiting for?

Some people work until they get to the point that they hate what they do. That is sad. When questioned, they often state that they always had a yearning to be doing something else. That is even sadder.

One of the most difficult things to grieve is the loss of a dream.

Do you wish that your business was different that it is now?

If so, schedule some quiet uninterrupted time when you can be creative. Take a couple of hours to write out a detailed description of what you would like your business to be like. There are no limits to what your imagination is allowed, so feel free to write out all your ideas - even if they seem impossible to accomplish.

Be very honest with yourself as you answer the following questions:

1. Should I consider expanding the business? What hours and days would I like to work? Would it make sense to develop partnerships or add staff to help reach my goals?

2. How could I change the business? Would it make sense to change the location? Is there training that would help me to move my practice into an area that I would enjoy more? Is there a client population that I would prefer to serve? How could I make this happen?

3. Should I make the business smaller? Am I working too many hours or preparing for retirement? Are there areas of practice that I would no longer like to do? Are there opportunities to maintain my income while reducing my investments of time and energy? Could I rent my office space to another business on a part-time or casual basis to replace hours when I will not be working?

4. Do I want to leave the business and do something different? What would an exit strategy look like? Would it be possible for someone else to take over the business? What other options do I have that are more attractive?

Former United States President Truman had a sign on his desk that read "The buck stops here". As a solo professional, the buck stops with you. You see, you have the option and responsibility to define your business and make the choices that will bring you to the end of your career with a smile on your face.

We grow when we volunteer

The organization called "Volunteering England" states:

> "We define volunteering as any activity that involves spending time, unpaid, doing something that aims to benefit the environment or someone (individuals or groups) other than, or in addition to, close relatives. Central to this definition is the fact that volunteering must be a choice freely made by each individual. This can include formal activity undertaken through public, private and voluntary organizations as well as informal community participation."

From the time I was a small child in rural Saskatchewan, I understood that volunteering is an important part of life. The first hamburger I ever cooked was in the curling rink. My mother had us setting up tables for church functions. We canvassed for charities and entertained at the nursing home.

Sometimes volunteering involves visiting with a shut-in, teaching an immigrant to speak English or coaching a sports team. Usually it requires a commitment which results in a life-changing experience for you and other people.

When I was in Atlanta, Georgia I visited the Jimmy Carter *Presidential Library and Museum*. President Carter's mother was known as "Miss Lillian". Her story is told in the book "First Mothers' by Bonnie Angelo and I will retell part of it using the information from that book.

When Mrs. Carter was 68 years of age she was a widow whose children had moved away from home. She was bored and feeling that she didn't have a purpose. She decided to apply to work as a volunteer in India through the Peace Corps.

She said, "I put in my application but I just knew the children were not going to let me go. It was a joke, me going to the Peace Corps - really ridiculous. But they let me down! .Nobody said 'Don't do it' so I had to go, you see, to keep from losing face with my children".

After two years, however, (when she was 70 years of age) she said that this was "the greatest thing that ever happened to me. It took two years out of my life but it was wonderful, the most meaningful experience of my life. I was so fulfilled".

And the results reached further than Miss Lillian might have imagined. Her son, Jimmy Carter, who is now in his 80s, continues to work diligently with *Habitat for Humanity* and his family members are volunteers in various activities.

You see volunteering is not just about you or the people you serve. It is also about your family and the example you set for them. Like a stone that is cast into a pond - there are ripple effects that influence those around you.

My grandparents were volunteers and my grandchildren are volunteers! It's intergenerational!

Are you a volunteer? Who is watching you? What are you doing in the world of volunteering that will help you to grow as an individual?

Life is a series of choices. Make good ones!

Recognize that we are all in this together!

I'm not a typical tourist who sits on the beach with a Margarita and this was evident during a trip that I made a few years ago to Jamaica.

I loaded my luggage with supplies for this third-world country and arranged to visit three schools and an orphanage to distribute them. Then I decided that it would be fun to visit Family Court!

Jamaica has a murder every thirty minutes and despite warnings about not leaving the resort, I hired a taxi and headed for the Court House. I was used to visiting Alberta government offices that feature expensive woods and rich upholstery. This was not the case with the Jamaican Court. I climbed the cement stairs outside the older building. The first floor housed used appliances and the second floor appeared to be used for storage. The third floor, my destination, held everything else - Probation, Counselling, Child Welfare, and Family Court.

As the "whitest" thing on the floor I quickly attracted attention. I asked for Mr. Green while showing my business card and birth certificate to the receptionist.

I had wondered if this name was some kind of a "code word" but was soon surprised to be ushered into the office of the CEO - a black man with a strong British accent who introduced himself to me as Mr. Green. Each chair in the room was filled with one of his staff members. Mr. Green apologized that he was not meeting me alone and explained "There are only two psychologists in all of Montego Bay and we don't have access to either". He immediately asked if I would teach him and provide a workshop for his people. We arranged for that to occur the following day.

In the meantime arrangements were made for me to be a visitor in Family Court. I was shocked at the surroundings and lack of resources. There were no electronics and the professionals who were in Court wrote all the proceedings by hand in large ledgers.

After Court and some waiting time the Judge approached me and asked "What were you writing in my Courtroom?" I had been using a small journal to record my observations but quickly said "All the things you were doing well". She smiled and invited me to her office to question me at length about various topics. Then she said "If I come early tomorrow will you come and teach me?" I agreed.

The following morning, Mr. Green came to the resort to get me. I met with the Judge again and afterwards Mr. Green apologized. He said "Ms. Hancock, you will hate me. We have so many crises in our region that I cannot bring my people in for a workshop. Shall I take you back to the resort?" My immediate reply was "Of course not. I committed to be here for the day so please put me to work".

What fun I had. I worked with a young man who had recently tried to burn down his mother's house, taught a Social Worker how to do a genogram and visited with the senior counsellor.

Once again I was surprised when there was a knock at the door and Mr. Green announced "The Minister of Justice has asked to meet you". Wow!

Ms. Smith, who I later learned was the head of the Department of Justice, and I talked and laughed and shared issues that were common to us. She then asked "Will you do a workshop for my people?"(they love workshops) and I agreed.

The reception area became my classroom as there was no other facility available and it was soon filled with paralegals, counselors and administrative staff. I turned to Ms. Smith and asked "What is the topic?" Without any hesitation she replied "Stress Management".

This experience reminded me that no matter what country we are in we all experience stress. Expectations are similar to the Olympic motto of "higher, faster and stronger". And reducing budgets mean that we are asked to do more with fewer resources. You see, learning to manage stress is a task that is not bound by geography, ethnicity or economics.

After the workshop Mr. Green indicated that he would drive me back to the resort. I was so touched when he said "Lady Hancock (formerly he had called me Ms. Hancock) I will always cherish this encounter. When you come to Jamaica again you will stay with my family and eat our food. We will show you Jamaica. And I will phone you and email you and do not be surprised when one day I arrive on your doorstep for I have so much to learn from you".

Well, I truly believe that I was the one who did the learning on that trip. The most important lesson that I learned was that we are all in this together. We are expected do more with less, to reach out to others who need us and sometimes we wonder how we will be able to carry on. Sometimes we become so focused on our own problems and issues that we forget we are just one part of a large and interconnected world.

But really the world is not all that big and some issues are universal. Because of this, it is very important that we reach out to encourage and help each other.

Take a moment each day to think about the work that is being done in other parts of the world. Can you make it easier for the workers? How can the choices you make in your life improve the situation for someone else? You see, just like a stone thrown into a pond, our actions ripple out to touch other people.

Perhaps you can also take a trip to another country and encourage those who, like you, face stress at times. My guess is that you will have a similar experience to the one I had – and that you will be the one who is truly blessed.

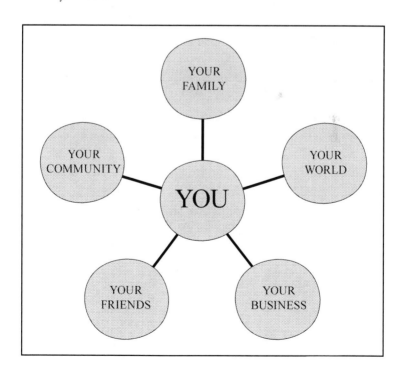

Dr. Linda Hancock

Three things we can promote to improve the world

The other day one of my clients stated that she would like to teach the three "R"s to people. My thoughts were that she was referring to "reading, 'riting and 'rithmetic" and I immediately began to wonder what had led her to say this as she wasn't a teacher. I was surprised when she went on to explain that her three "R"s consisted of "Respect", "Responsibility" and "Return to Common Sense".

My client demonstrated some real wisdom:

Respect needs to be a global attitude that includes respect for self, others, and the things of our world. When a person has self-respect, s/he is less inclined to fall into unhealthy activities or relationships. Instead, the person tends to learn about personal needs and endeavors to have those met in a positive manner. Respecting others facilitates communication, empathy and sharing. It reduces abuse and discrimination while fostering a spirit of collaboration. Respect for things of the world prevents pollution, waste of resources and property of others. It also acknowledges each country and culture as valuable.

Responsibility is a word that implies obligation and dependability. We must be responsible for ourselves - to do our work, care for others and act in a mature manner. It means that we do what we say that we will do and hold others accountable for what they promise to do.

Return to common sense is an interesting concept. Common sense isn't all that common anymore and it certainly doesn't make sense to everyone! The term implies that people should have practical answers to everyday situations. But we do not develop this ability unless we have a good example to follow or opportunities to learn through experience.

Planning Your Success

❑ Would you describe yourself as being Well-Seasoned?

❑ How can you simplify things?

❑ Do you take care of your health?

❑ What strategies can you use to balance work and home?

❑ What do you want from your business?

❑ Do you know the things that will help you to enjoy your work?

❑ What would you define as an appropriate income?

❑ Could you schedule travel for business and pleasure?

❑ Are there family members who could work with you?

❑ How might you expand or change your business in the future?

❑ What types of volunteering might you consider doing?

❑ Do you believe that globally we are all in this together?

❑ Are you committed to improving the world?

❑ What is the first business task you will do tomorrow morning?

Notes:

Epilogue

Shortly after I started writing this book, I realized that much of the content was going to be of a technical nature and therefore wanted to "lighten it up" a bit. My first thought was to add cartoons and I began to do some research. For hours I became lost by all the options that "Google" provided.

I knew what I wanted but really didn't know how to describe it.

Then I saw the website for Randy Glasbergen and realized that my search was over. I immediately fell in love with his characters and sense of humour. The research had paid off!

Now that the book is done I have thought about the process which has taught me two very important lessons.

As you are building your business you might not be able to describe exactly what you need - but you will recognize it once you find it. It is important, therefore, that you search until this occurs.

Secondly, you need to incorporate humour into both your personal life and your business life. I know people who have built large and prosperous enterprises who are very unhappy. I also know people who have few assets or resources who are extremely happy. It's not about what you have. It's about how you view things.

"Open for Business Success" would not be complete without this epilogue for it reminds and encourages all of us to continually search for the things we need and to laugh as we experience this wonderful adventure that we call "life".

Acknowledgements

Life is not lived in isolation and this book was not the work of one person. In fact, it is a compilation of the experiences that I have had throughout my lifetime and the influences of hundreds of individuals.

Over the years I have worked as an employee in public and private sectors as well as being a volunteer for local, provincial and national charitable organizations. Each experience has allowed me insight into the various ways that people accomplish tasks and work together, sometimes for the benefit of the owner and sometimes for the benefit of the group members who are involved. This has given me opportunity to learn a global perspective and various aspects of how the pieces of a large project are put together to achieve success.

Besides laying out the goals to fit a mandate, putting the resources in place and then operationalizing everything, I have learned the importance of budgeting, evaluation and showing appreciation for others.

Whenever someone works within an organization, that person learns personal skills that can be used in various arenas. Sometimes, what might seem to be even the most casual statement can appear as wisdom or the solution to a previously-unsolved problem.

Learning occurs in many ways. It might be obtained through a workshop, or from reading a book or from observing a mentor. It can appear in the answer to a well-formed question asked of another person or in the quiet that one experiences when thinking through an issue. It can happen through interaction with a senior, or a child or even a pet.

Throughout the years I have had good supervisors, peers and mentors who gifted me with their ideas. Co-workers have also helped me to broaden my knowledge base. Clients have been invaluable in refining my ideas and helping me to understand their situations. It is more than forty years since I entered the workforce and I am thankful for each day as they each offered valuable lessons.

My friends have been my friends not just because we share similar interests, but also because we care enough to help each to other grow. That requires honesty, patience and forgiveness.

It has been interesting to watch my children, Rob, Kristal and Mark grow up and begin their own careers and businesses. At times, they have asked me for advice about their challenges or goals. I too have learned from them and am thankful that our support goes both ways.

Now I benefit from six interesting grandchildren. They are excellent teachers who offer simple but profound lessons that are laced with a combination of innocence and genius.

You see, there isn't just one person to thank for their contributions to this book. There are many. I acknowledge each in my heart.

The knowledge and strategies found on these pages are all ones which I have personally adopted for my own businesses. My hope is that you will not merely read this book but that you will treasure it as a resource which you can refer to over and over again.

The time has come and be assured that beginning today you are now "Open for business success".

Linda

Make sure you have other

great products by Dr Linda:

www.LindaHancock.com

One of Linda's most requested keynote addresses is "Life is an Adventure" in which she combines her personal experiences, extensive work history and academic training into a hilarious but thought-provoking message. Its popularity has led to her first book and other resources with the same title.

Invite Dr. Linda to
your next event.

About the Author

L inda Hancock was born and raised in the prairie town of Indian Head, Saskatchewan, Canada. Following high school graduation, she worked in various administrative positions and was an extremely active mother of three children.

Linda earned degrees in Arts, Social Work, Education and Psychology to the Doctoral level. (As she says, she had to spend her time and money on something, because she doesn't golf!)

As a Registered Psychologist and Registered Social Worker, Dr. Hancock helps individuals, groups, organizations and communities to problem-solve and reach their potential. She is a trained mediator and arbitrator who has worked as a Child Welfare Case Manager and Investigator, Mental Health Consultant, and educator teaching in college and university settings. Her professional career has spanned the fields of justice, health and education.

Linda is a communicator. She speaks professionally, serves as a consultant for media personnel, and is also a published writer and columnist for two newspapers. She has given presentations at annual meetings, fundraising dinners, and community events for professionals, businesses, students and school personnel. She has also prepared and provided workshops for organizations and groups across North America and in Jamaica.

Throughout the years Linda has served as a volunteer on several local, provincial and national committees and boards. She is also a musician and she treasures every moment that she can be with her grandchildren.

Philosophy
To live
and learn
and love
in a manner that will lead to personal growth
and enhance the lives of others.

My Goal
is to encourage
individuals, groups, organizations,
and communities to reach their potential!